MOVIE VIEWER
Extraordinaire

DISCERNING THE INFLUENCES OF MOVIES ON YOUR FREEDOM, FAMILY AND HAPPINESS

TERI HAUX

ISBN: 1-4392-1485-9
ISBN-13: 9781439214855

Visit www.booksurge.com to order additional copies.

For Kelly, Porter, Savannah and Gavin.

Acknowledgements
I would like to thank my editors: Mary Wentz, Cynthia Behunin, Kelly S. Haux and Tina Adams. I also express my deepest gratitude to my Savior, Jesus Christ, for Divine guidance and daily inspiration.

CONTENTS

Magical Movies
CHAPTER ONE

I love movies. I love watching beautifully crafted stories in a dark theater where the atmosphere drowns all cares of the world. My mood brightens in anticipation as the lights finally dim and the opening credits run. Famous battles, individual triumphs, and outlandish fables flash across the screen pulling me into worlds exotic to mundane as stories not only unfold in front of my eyes but seemingly *from* my eyes as if I were living in the story. This is the magic.

It's not just me either. Watching movies has become one of the greatest national past-times ever. Every weekend millions of people sit in theaters all over the country, watching the same movies. Beyond reflecting our society, they have become our culture, complete with its own ceremonies. While the Druids of old worshipped according to the movement of the sun, moon and stars, we anxiously chart the calendar for new releases, dress up as characters, stand in long lines for tickets, pay exorbitant prices for popcorn and sodas, (which in superseding tradition, seems strangely like a sacrament) and cram into stuffy theaters with strangers to share in the ritual of story. Next we buy the DVD to experience the story in our homes and cars. It becomes part of our identity.

In addition to being a huge fan of cinema, I have spent the better part of a decade developing my craft as a screenwriter. Through these efforts of studying both sides of the screen, I have gained a deep appreciation and comprehension of the emotional significance associated with the whole cinematic experience. The first step to becoming an extraordinary movie viewer is to understand the basics of what makes a good movie and how movies use our feelings to affect us.

All movies are not created equal. Some unexpectedly bomb, while others attract growing attendance every week. As an audience member, there is a whole range of emotional and entertainment values we experience. Generally the movies that we enjoy the most have similar, predictable elements. First, for movies to be successful the audience must identify with the main character. The classic screenwriting book *Story*, by Robert McKee, explains that an audience empathizes with the protagonist because there's something in the character that strikes a chord with us. Unconsciously we think: "This character is like me. Therefore I want him to have whatever he wants because if I were in those circumstances, I'd want the same thing."

Movies impact our lives through this connection. We feel the characters' longings, triumphs and heartbreaks as if they were our own. It is because of this identification with the characters that movies work. It is what makes us laugh at comedies and cry while watching dramas; if we could not see ourselves as the protagonist it's not nearly as funny, sad or inspiring. We feel the same emotions the characters portray, making us laugh, weep or rise with anger at an injustice. Then, if the film's good, it sets everything right in the end.

The other main ingredient for successful films is the suspension of disbelief. McKee explains it this way,

> Two principles control the emotional involvement of an audience: identification with the protagonist that draws us into the story, vicariously rooting for our own desires in life. Second, authenticity: we must believe, or as Samuel Taylor Coleridge suggested, we must willingly suspend our disbelief…. We know that story telling is a ritual for life. To enjoy this ceremony we react to stories as if they're real.

The suspension of disbelief works by the unconscious shutting down of the critical portion of our brain which analyzes everything and exposing the emotional side of our minds.

A documentary on the life cycle of an earthworm would be viewed with the "thinking" part, even more so if it was a school assignment. Mental notes would be made on the names and phases of the earthworm's life. On the opposite end of this spectrum are our passions and feelings. Once this portion is cracked open, our minds accept the unbelievable. George Lucas, a master in the art of suspension of disbelief, begins the movie *Star Wars*, "A long time ago, in a galaxy far, far away." In our minds we think, okay this is not like our world; I wonder what this world is like. Instantly the critical part of the brain shuts down, and the emotions take over. However if Lucas had started the movie with "Last year, in a barnyard in East Texas…" we would be shaking our heads through the whole film going, thinking "that's not real." Even if movies are set in fantastic locations that we know are entirely imagined, if the characters behave in a believable manner, where their feelings and motivations are what the audience imagines they would feel in those situations, then we easily submit to the cinematic journey.

Walter Murch, a renowned film editor, puts this spin on it in his book *In the Blink of an Eye*,

> Whereas a good film that is well-edited seems like an exciting extension and elaboration of the audience's own feelings and thoughts, and they will therefore give themselves to it, as it gives itself to them.

Without the connection to the protagonist or suspension of disbelief, movies remain on a cognitive level along with school or work. But effective movies lead us to experience emotions that can touch us on the deepest levels of our being, our hearts and souls, and put us in touch with our humanity. We go to the movies to learn about ourselves.

∽

Before the cinema splashed into our cultural landscape around one hundred years ago, books held a greater amount of influence in the lives of Americans. When our country was first founded, the national vibe was firmly rooted in the Bible which the majority of American families read. This facilitated a similar dialog throughout the States; all events in daily life and written reports were viewed through the same paradigm as the Bible. Stealing, lying, swearing and adultery were all bad. Helping a neighbor was a given. This is not to say that life was perfect but that the moral compass that judged between good and bad was clearly defined.

Sadly, this is no longer the case. Movies filled with subversive messages and dubious heroes have surpassed books, namely the Bible, as the overriding pulse generator. They define how we relate to others. Because they can affect us so deeply, movies more easily plant feelings that can lead to actions. This is particularly true of children who are still deciphering the ways of life.

Cinema also creates the dialog of interaction. Children and adults use movies to relate to friends. It's literally a litmus test for compatibility. "Did you see the latest *Spiderman* (or Barbie or Jackie Chan) film? Me too." A conversation of movies or TV shows between two individuals is really a discussion of feelings and a method of quickly identifying compatibility. "I feel this way because I watch these movies, and if you like the same ones, we must feel the same way."

> **Movies based on Biblical events have been some of the most influential and important pictures Hollywood has ever produced. Great films like *The Passion (2004)*, *Ben Hur* (1959) and *The Ten Commandments* (1956) inspire and instruct in their beautiful presentations of pure truths that are felt as much as learned.**

One of my college professors began her relationship with her future husband when he was the only person at a large party to agree with her that the infamous driving off the cliff scene in *Thelma and Louise* (1991) was the only possible way it could've ended. When there is discordance in the types of movies enjoyed, it may be more difficult to find common ground for a friendship. The conversation of how we feel about particular films effectively results in a genesis of friendship, cooperation or the recognition of incompatibility. Movies are the carrier by which we can engage in discussions regarding our true feelings without actually revealing them as such perhaps even to ourselves.

Feelings define us as individuals. Often we feel things before we can define them cognitively. The runaway best-selling book, *The Secret*, goes even further. Through essays from various professionals, it implies that our feelings and desires create our reality. In that book, Marci Shimoff explains, "Our feelings let us know what we are thinking." Feelings are an integral part of the movie experience, which in turn have the very real power to influence our lives on very personal levels.

As viewers, we should learn to recognize the messages imbedded in this medium in order to maintain our personal area of influence. The main weapon movies use to influence us is our feelings. In 388 BC, Plato urged city leaders to exile all story-tellers and poets on the grounds that they were a threat to society. He argued that "they conceal ideas inside the seductive emotions of art." He further explained that felt ideas are ideas nonetheless, and "The persuasive power of a story is so great that we may believe its meaning even if we find it morally repugnant." In other words, the emotions and thoughts experienced while entranced in a story are just as real as if someone was living through the same episode. The multimedia presentations we have today are exponentially more engaging and therefore more powerful precisely because they engage our emotions.

Feelings are intensely personal and undeniable. They are part of our souls; even after death, they remain with us, along with our intellect. Our desires, hopes, dreams and heartache truly define us as individuals. Furthermore, feelings, emotions and thoughts experienced during a movie are just as authentic and valid as those felt outside the theater. The mind does not distinguish between the two. Dr. Denise Waitely explains in the book *The Secret*, Olympic athletes' brains were monitored during actual training and during a visualization of their training; the results were identical "Because the mind can't distinguish whether you're really doing it or it's just a practice." The brain reacts identically to stimulus, real or imagined.

This has a far-reaching implication in the media industry where, in addition to reality-approaching technology, movie makers and screen writers deliberately seek to engage the viewer's feelings on the deepest level possible. McKee coaches film industry writers on their craft in *Story* by explaining "The audience must not just understand; it must believe. You want the world to leave your story convinced that yours is a true metaphor for life." The whole movie presentation is planned in every step of production to control what the audience feels in each scene, shot and frame. Cinema is as much of an emotional experience as a visual feast.

When I was a nanny some years ago, I accompanied my young charge, Kyle, to watch *Beauty and the Beast* (1991). I had previewed the Disney animated film, and it seemed appropriate for a four-year-old. Yet the scenes where the beast fights with the wolves absolutely terrified him. He was sobbing hysterically. Walking with him into the hall of the theater, I tried to calm him by assuring him that there was nothing to be afraid of and that it was just a movie. But he was inconsolable. I had a choice of forcing him back into a movie he emphatically resisted or leaving mid-show. I drove him home. During the next two years that I remained his nanny he would never watch that movie. Was he experiencing fake fear? Absolutely not. They were his real feelings.

On another occasion, I was thirty minutes early for a matinee, so I decided to pop into *Walk the Line* (2005) with Reese Witherspoon. I had time to kill, and I wasn't sure if I wanted to see it. I slipped into the seat nearest the exit, wearing my coat and holding my purse in my lap. I thought I would only be there for a moment. Then the movie started and my plans disintegrated. I couldn't move from that spot. Cemented in a terrible seat, clutching my coat and purse, I was utterly entranced through the entire show. It was magic. I felt the despair, the hope, the drive to continue and the love that the characters felt. I believed this film portrayed accurate emotions, reactions and consequences for the individuals in the story. I was emotionally committed. Even after the show, I continued to feel the catharsis and healing.

More amazing to me, however, was when I first watched *Crouching Tiger, Hidden Dragon* (2000). I was utterly entranced in the characters and their gravity defying motion. It seemed so natural and believable, not at all like the cheesy visions of Superman being lifted on cables with poorly done back drops. I felt they were really soaring through the air, even though my brain knows they also had cables suspending them. It felt so real to me that I vividly recall the stinging disappointment when I walked out of the theater and realized that I couldn't fly.

Movies in general are enticing and highly entertaining, but they are NOT two hours of mindless entertainment as many in the industry today would have you believe. In the 1930's a group of Hollywood executives made this self regulating statement explaining the organization of the Motion Picture Association of America (MPAA):

> Motion pictures producers recognize the high trust and confidence which have been placed in them by the people of the world.... They recognize their responsibility to the public because of this trust and because entertainment and art are important influences in the life of a nation.

In today's climate of permissiveness in film, statements from executives sound more like disclaimers, but at one point officials in the industry did publically acknowledge their influential role in our society.

Part of this power and influence results from the fact that movie theaters are so similar to classrooms. Both involve a group of people all facing the same direction listening and watching a presentation. As a society in general, this is how we have been trained to receive instruction. They are nearly identical rituals; the effects are similar as well. Both result in the transmission of facts, ideas and feelings. However, rarely are traditional classroom subjects presented on celluloid and school attendance is compulsory. Children in school often need encouragement to follow the rules which dictate they sit in one seat for fort-five minutes at a stretch, yet the same child will pay to sit for three straight hours watching the latest Harry Potter flick. Why? Movies are the study of life. We watch them to learn about ourselves through the actions and dreams of other people. This is great as long as the cinematic lessons are at least compatible with our personal and religious morals. Tragedy follows, though, when susceptible minds seize upon incorrect and immoral examples to emulate.

Aristotle worried about these very ideas regarding stories.

In "The Poetics" he reasons, "For to imitate is congenial to men from childhood. And in this they differ from animals, that they are most imitative, and acquire the first disciplines through imitation; and that all men delight in imitations."

He continues,

"But since imitators imitate those who do something, and it is necessary that these should either be worthy or depraved persons.... By this very same difference, also, tragedy differs from comedy. For one seeks to imitate worse, but the other better men than they are."

The lifestyles in current cinema exhibit no restraint on the depths humanity can possibly be shown to plunge. Imagine the harm and destruction that would come to our children if murder, cannibalism, torture, occultism, adultery and blasphemy were subjects taught in school. Yet this is what people study in many movies, where everyone is a student and the stakes are much higher than academic ratings; this filth is aimed at our soul.

Although adults don't easily succumb to overt attacks on core beliefs, no one is immune. Young children are extremely vulnerable mainly because their limited life-experience leaves them less able to discern between beneficial and harmful visions for life. Additionally, they often will watch the same movie over and over. I first noticed this as a nanny; Shiloh, age two, was obsessed with *The Little Mermaid* (1989). She watched the movie every day, at least once, sang the songs throughout the day and wore her Ariel swimsuit without fail–rain, sun or snow. At first I thought this behavior was odd, but when my own children (who couldn't possibly be odd) fixated on certain movies as well (*Toy Story* (1995) and *Princess Bride* (1987)), I realized that it must be the standard operating procedure for young children. Nearly every other mother I have spoken with about this subject can tell you which movie their children preferred. Psychologists explain that there are two reasons for this: the predictability comforts them and they are learning about life. I add that we are all learning about life: children, youth and adults.

Life is full of emotions of every kind: tragedy, success, love, hate–they create the texture and color in life. This is doubly true for movies, where heightened feelings and situations draw the audience into the characters in the short span of a few minutes. Through movies we vicariously, yet just as tangibly to our brains and spirits, pass through sorrow as well as other emotions and return home better able to recognize them. Feelings and emotions are the key within the framework of a plausible reality.

Movies which are emotionally benign are forgettable at best; often they leave viewers irritated that they wasted their two hours and twenty or so dollars. Next there are movies that elicit feelings that contradict our basic core beliefs, such as the notion that killing people is entertaining and a good solution to problems. These travesties against humanity are generally easy to weed out though before we plunk down our cash for a ticket. The most dangerous type of films are the ones that appear to be pleasant entertainment but place small falsehoods and violate morals in slight and often confusing ways. This is what the majority of the chapters of this book will focus on.

The reason we do not abandon film entirely is for the last type of movie, the pure gems that leave us with transcendent feelings of hope for all humanity and inner happiness; movies that hold our breath and take us on an emotional journey so profound that we find ourselves unable even to blink until after the credits roll–the magical movies. Unfortunately, they are rarer than diamonds, and a plethora of ersatz efforts cloud the field. The purpose of this book is to help you discern which movies will be suitable for you and your families in order to minimize the damage that undesirable movies could have by revealing the methods and implications of agendas, hidden and overt.

The FCC Chairman Newton Minnow elaborated in 1966, "The power of instantaneous sight and sound is without precedent in mankind's history. This is an awesome power. It has limitless capabilities for good—and evil. And it carries with it awesome responsibilities." The burden to distinguish the messages of this great power lies on our own shoulders. No one else is doing it for us, and there are people who would use this medium to harm our society and personal sovereignty. Additionally this is a privilege we should willingly embrace which is derived from the precious and fragile freedom we enjoy in our great nation. We can make our own choices; therefore, we should.

Influencing Society through Entertainment

CHAPTER TWO

Current movie executives may never publically admit the extent that movies influence society. They depend upon the perception of triviality in order to maintain the power of persuasion over unsuspecting masses. Influence, which every group and individual trying to alter the status quo craves as they actively pursue as much screen time as possible. Currently there are numerous entities who seek to use the most powerful media ever created for their own purposes. Movie executives know movies effectively influence society in deep and subtle ways. In order to quell harmful influences which may come through the cinema, we must understand the many ways manipulation is being used and who is regulating it. These efforts range from simple product placement by advertising companies, to executives in the industry who are vehemently fighting any efforts aimed at minimizing harmful elements of their "art", followed by factions of our government who are trying to enact laws aimed at controlling the content of the media.

Buying Consumer Influence

My first inkling of the power of the silver screen was through one of my screenwriting courses in college. My professor explained that the movie *Saturday Night Fever* (1977) altered the entire cotton industry when John Travolta strutted his coolness without a t-shirt under his wide-collared flashy shirt. As people everywhere emulated his attire, sales of standard white tees, a staple in the 1950s, plummeted. Factories with fewer orders made cutbacks, decreasing the demand for raw cotton from farmers. All this snowballed from one character in a single movie. I'm sure the filmmakers had not planned this, but it happened nonetheless.

More often products on screen aim to increase sales. In another notable example, M&Ms refused the product placement opportunity in the classic children's movie *E.T.* (1982) Reeses Pieces then jumped at the opportunity to be the candy the character Elliot uses to make a trail to lure the alien to his home. Reeses candy sales spiked in conjunction with the release of the film and has remained steady ever since, boosting it to the status of a permanent fixture in the candy aisle at nearly every food and convenience store.

It is interesting to note that many movie executives sell product placements for huge sums of money because everyone involved in the production process believes, with good reason, that advertising in this manner is very effective. At the same time they deny any responsibility for promoting "bad" behavior in movies. Michael Medved explains this phenomenon exceptionally eloquently in his book, *Hollywood vs. America,* while referring to the small screen:

> It is the height of hypocrisy that the same network executives who accept—and demand—this lavish payment for the briefest moments of broadcast advertising simultaneously try to convince us that their many hours of programming do nothing to change the attitudes of the audience. In short they have adopted the outrageously illogical assumption that a sixty-second commercial makes a more significant impression than a sixty-minute sitcom.

This holds doubly true for the big screen where the images and sounds are literally larger than life. Every aspect of the cinema leaves an impression with the audience. There are many groups and individuals who seek to usurp power and influence through this slight of hand persuasion by maintaining complete control of its messages.

Controlling Movie Messages

One casualty of this battle is the company Clean Flicks, which, along with other similar companies, sold and rented edited versions of Hollywood's biggest hits. They operated by buying one copy of a movie, altering it and selling the sanitized version, with a one-to-one ratio. The production houses still collected a royalty for every unit sold and customers could enjoy movies without compromising their values. It seemed like a fair business plan since most movies go through the editing process anyway when they air on cable TV, airplanes and some foreign markets. This good-intentioned, small company, however, was vehemently attacked by film industry goliaths like Steven Spielberg and Disney in the courts for changing the director's "artistic vision." Many comments in the blogs and news reports expressed wonder at why film industry giants would desire to close down a business that was reaching new customers. Financially, it doesn't make sense for an industry which survives by selling a product (movies) to legally intervene in order to block sales to one entire market. The impetus for their assault is one that trumps dollars—power and influence.

In order to understand, the facts should be examined closely. Clean Flicks maintained a customer base who wanted to purchase movies but were opposed to certain degrading elements. Clean Flicks removed the offensive material to make some movies more palatable for their customers. The industry behemoths fought to keep the most abhorrent components included. Through massive litigation they tried to force people to view scenes that violate their morals. This is a direct attack on conservative America. The proof is in the accounting.

The Secular Progressives (Bill O'Reilly's term for people that seek to destroy America's conservative tradition) that fill the ranks of Hollywood tow the same liberal line as their elected associates. One political battle that spills into entertainment venues is the push to reenact the Fairness Doctrine. While this has a pleasant, non-threatening name it actually amounts to pure intimidation of media outlets. The broad terms state that any person or small group that is attacked in a limited media, like TV or radio, personally is entitled to free air time to respond. The Fairness Doctrine was originally an FCC policy, not a federal regulation. The position of self-imposed guidelines surpassed its intended realm when, in 1969, the Supreme Court ruled in favor of the FCC enforcing this doctrine in the case against Red Lion Co, regarding a Christian radio broadcast that criticized the book, *Goldwater: Extremist of the Right*, without giving the author, James Cook, time to rebut the attack. The web site for The Museum of Broadcast Communications explains the effect this way:

> The doctrine, nevertheless, disturbed many journalists, who considered it a violation of First Amendment rights of free speech/free press which should allow reporters to make their own decisions about balancing stories. Fairness, in this view, should not be forced by the FCC. In order to avoid the requirement to go out and find contrasting viewpoints on every issue raised in a story, some journalists simply avoided any coverage of some controversial issues. This "chilling effect" was just the opposite of what the FCC intended.

The net effect was that stations were bullied by threat of lawsuit not to broadcast anything controversial or that implicated any wrongdoing by individuals. President Reagan is the hero here though. The FCC chairman he appointed ended the FCC policy. Liberal lawmakers took up its banner and passed legislation that would make censorship-under-the-guise-of-fairness a bona fide law. And Reagan vetoed it. The following president, George H.W. Bush, did the same thing.

The fight is not over. The previous use of the Fairness Doctrine to sue a conservative Christian radio show illustrates clearly who the target is for ongoing efforts to restore the ill conceived regulation. This policy that became pseudo-law through circumventing voters Secular Progressives tout as a weapon against religion and morals. Congressional Representative (D-OH) Dennis Kucinich, along with other liberals, has proposed that this program be reinstated. Senator John Kerry explained, as quoted in The Limbaugh Letter, that if The Fairness Doctrine had been law, he would've been elected instead of George W. Bush.

Another political battle that leaks into the media realm is Net Neutrality, in which the liberals in the Legislative branch of government want to create regulations for the internet that ban anyone from limiting or favoring access to any online applications. The problems that Net Neutrality would seem to be fixing are not based on actual problems consumers are reporting only speculative issues. Besides creating unnecessary government meddling, the biggest effect of any Net Neutrality law would be to tie the hands of companies that filter undesirable content for consumers. In other words, they want to disable any tools that allow families to block access to pornography.

Political battles may seem far away from the thousands of movie screens in our beautiful country, but there are a few key points. The Secular Progressives hold nothing sacred in their battles against regular Sunday-go-to-church Americans. These are the same type of organizations that the ultra-liberal Hollywood Elite endorse. Also, it does not matter if famous personalities officially support harmful organizations, like Oliver Stone, a famous film director who is a member of the American Humanist Association, (which seeks to eliminate Bibles and Qurans from courts and further world views based solely on science) and those whose performances and productions support similar anti-conservative stances.

Many prominent people in the film industry proclaim their political (Socialist) ideals passionately and use their celebrity status to gain attention for whatever agenda they endorse. The critical point here is that their very outspoken nature would almost guarantee that every project they work on would reiterate their political positions. We are no more likely to see Jane Fonda or George Clooney make a movie supporting the American Government than the Supreme Court overturn Roe v. Wade because they realized they had overstepped their power.

Political influence in our movies is analogous to the current public school systems and its debate for vouchers for children to attend private schools. The Secular Progressives in the legislative branch are fighting viciously to prevent vouchers from going to lower income children to enable them to attend private schools.

In each of these cases gaining control is overriding motivation: influencing what we buy, watch in movies, learn in school and which political opinions are allowed broadcast time. Even this small sampling of competing persuasions proves that we cannot enter blindly into the huge world of media. The first step is learning to recognize propaganda in all its forms so we can make a conscious choice in all our decisions. Gone is the day when we could enjoy entertainment without worry. We must scrutinize what we partake of in the media especially because of the extensive agendas being sold to us as amusement by the film executives, private companies and even some in our own government.

Historical Manipulation
CHAPTER THREE

From the moment we step out of bed in the morning until we collapse into deep sleep from the stresses of the day, we are surrounded by choices. Most choices are easy. Picking the candy of our choice in the supermarket aisle is as harmless as it seems. Other choices, such as our personal value system and who to marry, carry far greater consequences, and maintain a higher degree of complexity over selecting our favorite sweets from the candy aisle at Walmart. However, there are groups and individuals who actively manipulate our choices through a sinister desire to control much more than product sales; they aggressively seek social and political power through the film industry. This is not a new phenomenon. Political spin doctors under the guidance of notorious dictators as well as benevolent democratic leaders all over the world have been using the arts to their shameless advantage for centuries.

One of the most infamous examples happened in the first quarter of the Nineteenth Century. In October 1917, the Communists, led by Vladimir Lenin and the Bolsheviks, eliminated the Czar monarchy which had ruled for over 300 years in a nearly bloodless coup. The last Czar, Nicholas I, mismanaged the government horribly. Peasants were starving and conscripted soldiers where dying by the ten thousands in World War I. Inflation wiped out the meager buying power of the Russian Ruble while food shortages made it nearly impossible to buy food regardless of financial resources. The extreme discontent of the general population opened the door for the drastic transformation of every aspect of Russian life.

The key ingredient in Lenin's grab for power in the floundering country was his propaganda. In 1922 he famously said, "Of all the arts for us the cinema was most important." He won the support of the illiterate peasants by parading enticing images that emulated his deceptive slogan of "Peace, Land, Bread." His movies showed happy farmers surrounded by healthy children with plenty to eat. The citizen's hope of emulating the prosperous life radiantly displayed in the movies was so powerful that the masses unquestioningly subscribed to Lenin's rule. It was easy for the Bolsheviks to create their images of outlandish lies in which the uneducated peasants could easily believe. All the filmmakers had to do was literally roll the cameras in one hand while aiming a rifle in the other.

The Bolshevik triumph in October was accomplished nine-tenths psychologically: the forces involved were negligible, a few thousand men at most in a nation of one hundred and fifty million, and victory came

almost without a shot being fired. The whole operation seemed to confirm Napoleon's dictum that the battle is won or lost in the minds of men before it even begins.
Richard Pipes, *The Russian Revolution*.

To maintain his authority, Lenin continued to use entertainment venues to subdue the population. Under his dictatorial rule, the arts flourished. There were theaters everywhere, supplied by a huge system of directors, actors and producers that created works on demand. For artists in Russia it was the golden years with work aplenty and throngs of patrons to fill the theaters' free seats. It is easy to think, "Wow", or "How generous," but coercing millions of people to abide by his authoritarian rule is not an act of kindness. This was business, and it had nothing to do with making money, as is proven by the accounting. Lenin needed the support of the people, whatever the financial cost.

The proletariat never experienced the better life that Lenin promised. The subsequent Russian Civil War which challenged Lenin's new government has come to be characterized not only by the millions of soldiers and civilians dead from violence, sickness and starvation, but also personal sorrow and hardship on an unimaginable scale.

The heyday for the arts in Russia abruptly halted when Josef Stalin seized power after Lenin's death. Stalin worried he couldn't control all of the messages being put forth, and his answer was to simply execute people in the film and theater industries. He believed they were a threat, and he had no compunction about cold-blooded murder. With the current treasonous trends in our own movie industry, his fears, though not his actions, seem logical.

Lenin was certainly not the only tyrant to control whole populations through the entertainment venues. Adolph Hitler and Joseph Goebbels, the master of Hitler's propaganda, micro-managed every aspect of the media during his totalitarian role in the 1930s and early 40s. German cinema perpetuated the lies that Jews were devious, subhuman, unfeeling and the root cause of all of Germany's problems. Hitler shut down every outlet that spoke against him or that supported the Jewish cause. They strictly supervised those that remained, effectively controlling every bit of information citizens might receive. Besides their own conscience, the German population had no reason to doubt the lies they were being fed.

During my study and preparation for writing a feature length script about Germany in World War II, I read numerous accounts from people who experienced this crisis. According to my research the average person was unaware of the fact that people were systematically being eradicated, sometimes even in their own towns. Many living in the Jewish ghettos had no idea of the fate awaiting them at the end of the train rides. Half of the battle the Resistance faced was convincing people of the stark reality, that only death awaited them if they submitted to the Nazi's. The other challenge was simply staying alive. This testifies to the effectiveness of Hitler's propaganda machine.

On our side of the pond political history intertwines with cinema as well, although with a vastly different purpose and outcome, at least so far. The birth of our own film industry began around the turn of the nineteenth century in New York. Thomas Edison, one of the key individuals involved, personified the entire group of elite protestant males running the business. Early silent films were meant to be frivolous amusement, but they always reinforced the social hierarchy the elites depended on. Blacks and Jews were shown as low class, unintelligent and dangerous.

Birth of a Nation (1915) epitomizes this idea. It shows the KKK saving a post-Civil War town, particularly the white women, from lustful freed slaves, by hanging the offenders. The effects of this movie were dramatic; riots broke out in many Midwest cities, some theaters refused to show it at all, one white man murdered a black teenager he saw in the street after watching it. The KKK, which was nearly extinct, made a giant recovery and according to Roger Ebert used this movie as a recruitment tool up until 1970.

However, while the Protestant elite headed movie productions and distributions, the majority of skilled workers were Jewish immigrants. They flocked to this burgeoning field because nearly all other respectable jobs in banking, academia and industry were closed to them due to their beliefs. When Jewish immigrants began to create their own films, Edison and other elite producers formed a monopoly, excluding them. In a quintessential American ideal, the immigrants picked up and moved to California where they created the Hollywood Film Industry. The six major studios were all headed by Jewish men from Eastern Europe. It is these men, Harry Warner, Carl Laemli, William Fox, Adolph Zucker, Louis Meyer and Samuel Goldwyn, who ironically created our current ideal for the perfect American society.

The immigrants wanted to be Americans, but they were excluded from Edison's world. To counter their exclusion by the Protestant elite they made their own version of America where they would fit in. In the early films of the Hollywood industry, the working class proved its mettle, different ethnic groups coexisted peacefully, mothers were lionized and the freedoms enjoyed in America were celebrated (For example any Jimmy Stewart movie). These ideals did not reflect contemporary society; they wanted to create it. In the end, Americans embraced the vision.

This influence was so profound U.S. government officials began to take note. In 1939 fighting broke out in Europe at the start of World War II, the U.S. government sent Joseph P. Kennedy, a former ambassador to Great Britain, to secretly meet with the studio heads in California. Kennedy warned the studio heads to stop making anti-fascist films, reasoning that if the U.S. did become involved in the war, people would blame them. His recommendations were heeded.

The attack on Pearl Harbor on December 7, 1941 changed everything. After the bombing and our inevitable entry into the War, the government had another request: patriotic movies. The studios jumped into overdrive, cranking out film after film that showed Americans as heroes in fighting tyranny. These inspiring films were shipped overseas to the fighting men where they were shown, twenty-four hours a day. The movies effectively impressed upon the soldiers what they were fighting for, which buoyed morale during their long struggle for victory and world peace.

The current climate in Hollywood has swung the other direction. Even though our nation has troops serving overseas and facing dangerous foes, movies are far more likely to show Americans as the enemy and glorify the oppressive opponents we face. This is not because our movie-goers are choosing to be anti-American, but because the Hollywood system is being controlled in order to create those feelings in our country.

A-list stars such as Sean Penn, Tim Robbins, Jane Fonda are all friends of Fidel Castro, the former Communist leader of Cuba. Castro embraces sympathizing U.S. movie stars at the same time he imprisons and executes any artist whom he feels does not conform to his dogma. With Castro's declining health, Hugo Chavez, the Communist dictator of Venezuela has come into vogue with some of Hollywood's brightest stars. Sean Penn received the royal treatment during a recent visit. Chavez praised Penn for his public call to impeach President George W. Bush. He and other liberals in Hollywood like Jane Fonda clearly favor Communist nations over our own and their attitudes are infiltrating the whole Hollywood system.

High profile visits to communist leaders from stars and fashion models, such as Naomi Campbell, try to make it popular to have socialistic ideals like: no national borders, universal healthcare, and asset redistribution. All of these notions don't sound so terrible if you're the underachiever looking for a handout. But upon closer examinations, the horrible implication is obvious: these notions are one step away from communism and miles away from ensuring our personal freedom.

This anti-American trend is so ingrained in the Hollywood system that it is nearly impossible to make a movie that shows otherwise. A biographical script I wrote about a reporter during the Vietnam Conflict who unabashedly supported the everyday soldiers didn't get past the readers. The reason given was although my script was realistic and entertaining it contradicted the current political environment in Hollywood, specifically Oliver Stone's version of Vietnam, in which our soldiers were drug-addicted baby killers.

I am not the only person to have a screenplay rejected because it is too conservative, regardless of quality. Hundreds of writers experience the same attitudes. Many of them give up trying to write screenplays, or they change what they are writing to cater to a system which seems to daily push the boundaries of propriety to new lows. When scripts with traditional values are green-lit by production houses they all too often are altered in order to present the political platforms of the Secular Progressives in charge.

One example of this obvious anti-American sentiment is the upcoming movie based on G.I. Joe action hero, an American soldier icon. Buenavista changed the whole concept and is now making a film about a group of Global soldiers who fight all over the world. According to pre-production buzz the film does not want to romanticize the American soldier, instead they celebrate a unified World culture.

The danger here is that movies are not reflecting how the majority of Americans feel or what they believe, but they are trying to alter it in a significant manner. Emulating the murderous tyrants of the twentieth century, their prize extends beyond political victories; they are after the very core of our society, our freedom. Of course Americans love their liberties, and will not easily give them up. So those who seek for this control are striking at an even more personal target so they can first weaken our citizens, the family.

Conspiracy Afoot
CHAPTER FOUR

Largely due to his masterful control of the arts, Vladimir Lenin was able to subdue over 150 million people and subject them to murderous rule. At the same time Lenin was binding his people to a yoke of cruelty and misery, the United States of America was growing and would eventually become the most affluent and powerful country in the world. It represents the crown jewel for anyone who seeks for world domination. It is beyond naïve to deny that there are people seeking for precisely that, however implausible it sounds. To have any hope of maintaining the sovereignty of America we must recognize methods that mimic those of the Russian Revolution in order to minimize or eliminate efforts in our entertainment venues that weaken our society through attacking families and create a dependence on social programs, which could lead to the same end.

Vladimir Lenin knew he could not have seized power from the Czar if the people were prosperous and peaceful. It was necessary to create an environment eliminating wealth and safety, a necessary precursor for populations to willingly give up their freedom. While it may seem cynical and unbelievable that any person or group would intentionally conspire to destroy centuries of Democracy, there is a documented history of just that.

As far back as the Eighteenth Century, a secret society called the Illuminati has been plotting to gain power of all the citizens of the world. In a manner similar to Lenin's, a system developed by the Illuminati involves directly assaulting the family in carefully planned out baby steps. William H. Mc Ilhany details the history of this conspiracy in an article, "Two Centuries of Intrigue" featured in the *New American* magazine in 1996. (How could I write about conspiracy and not refer to the *New American*?) He explains the origins of the Illuminati. Adam Weishaupt purportedly led a group of 13 founding families starting in Bavaria, Germany. This vile group had aspirations to rule the world through detailed plans which span generations. (No one can confirm that they are NOT still pursuing their goals.) Members of the Illuminati sought for positions which could influence government policy and sway public opinion, such as advisors to kings and religious figures. Weishaupt was a professor of Cannon at Ingolstadt University, and by 1778, two years after the order was founded, all but two of the department chairs at Ingolstadt belonged to members of his society. Mc Ilhany states:

> The original writings of the Order included detailed instructions for fomenting hatred and bloodshed

between different racial, religious, and ethnic groups—and even between the sexes. The idea of promoting hatred between children and their parents was introduced. There were even instructions about the kinds of buildings to be burned in urban insurrections. In short, virtually every tactic employed by 20th-century subversives was planned and written down by Adam Weishaupt over 200 years ago.

They successfully endeavored to make divorce easier and more appealing by mocking the sanctity of marriage via labeling it a man made institution based on prejudice that harms and binds people. Their agenda included ways to gain influence over the youth, and supplant the guidance and nurturing from parents with their own falsehoods.

The Illuminati's ultimate goal is a world-wide socialistic society without any national borders, where they are in charge of everything and everyone. They are not content with being extravagantly

The United States government does not make our currency or coin, the Federal Treasury does. The name gives the impression of a government agency, but it is actually a privately owned company. President Wilson approved this arrangement and signed off on the legislation, but later lamented that he had been the means of undoing our freedom and republic, because whoever controls the usury has the real power.

wealthy and ensconced away on their private estates. They want to prevent other people from achieving greatness and prosperity. When people are financially secure and independent, they are not as easily controlled. It's not ultimately about money, though, it is about power. They control all the big banks, such as the Chase and Morgan institutions, and the Federal Treasury, where they can literally print their own money.

J. P. (John Pierpont) Morgan, one of America's wealthiest financiers and a member of one of the rumored families that control the Illuminati, stated in a private communiqué to leading U.S. Bankers in 1934:

> Capital must protect itself in every way.... Debts must be collected and loans and mortgages foreclosed as soon as possible. *When through a process of law the common people have lost their homes, they will be more tractable and more easily governed by the strong arm of the law applied by the central power of leading financiers.* People without homes will not quarrel with their leaders. This is well known among our principle men now engaged in forming an imperialism of capitalism to govern the world. *By dividing the people we can get them to expend their energies in fighting over questions of no importance to us except as teachers of the common herd.* (emphasis added)

The implications of this attitude are unthinkable. The Illuminati and other power-hungry Socialists want families to lose their homes and to manipulate the world according to their whimsical fantasies, not to bring happiness or world peace or any other benevolent ideal, but to subject all citizens to their rule, through financial control. After the October Russian Revolution, Lenin accomplished this mandate as soon as he came into power. The people actually celebrated as the government seized the property of ALL the landowners. This move effectually eliminated any threat that may have come from the potentially influential land barons. Before perishing on Korean Airlines flight 007, which was shot down by the Soviet Union on September 1, 1983, Larry P. McDonald, U.S. Congressman, explains it clearly, as quoted in *The Rockefeller File*, by Gary Allen.

> The drive of the Rockefellers and their allies is to create a one-world government combining supercapitalism and Communism under the same tent, all under their control.... Do I mean conspiracy? Yes I do. I am convinced there is such a plot, international in scope, generations old in planning, and incredibly evil in intent.

There is enough evidence to warrant consideration. Our freedom is too precious to blindly allow possible secret combinations to threaten it.

❧

Lenin is not the only Communist leader to have conquered a large nation; Mao Tse Tung also used similar tactics from the Illuminati handbook in his takeover of China. First he removed mothers from their home. One point in his book of quotations states: "Enable every woman who can work to take her place on the labor front.... This should be done as quickly as possible." This accomplished many objectives, namely, it freed the youth from parental supervision and the labor the mothers performed enhanced Chairman Mao's empire and at the same time reduced the labor that benefitted each respective household. Wives and mothers were no longer managing domestic duties including child rearing, cooking, cleaning and shopping; their life's energy was enriching the government instead of their families.

With absent parents, children were more easily enticed into joining the Red Guard which patrolled their neighborhoods and homes reporting any offenses of the new "Cultural Revolution." Parents and other elders were afraid of the youth, who could report them to the authorities. To further sever familial connections all historical genealogies were ordered to be destroyed. No longer were parents dreams and morals passed down to their children. Instead children's minds were filled with Chairman Mao's goals, which had nothing to do with personal happiness or fulfillment. The regime that Mao created decades ago still stands as a testament to the effectiveness of his methods.

We face this same threat in our society, although not from a government mandate, but from pressure in the media.

> The sentimental veneration of motherhood… could never quite obscure the reality that unpaid labor bears the stigma of social inferiority when money becomes the universal measure of value.
> Christopher Lasch, *Revolt of the Elites*

In other words, when the dollar is the yardstick by which worth is calculated, the perceived value of stay at home mothers plummets compared to working mothers. The pendulum has swung so far that mothers who stay at home bear a stigma similar to that of unwed mothers in previous generations. When all of the entertainment industry glorifies the appearance of wealth and fame, a parent's selfless use of time and talents in raising children is utterly devalued.

Lasch elaborates on the consequences of having both parents in the workplace stating children are vulnerable outside influences.

> The television set becomes the principle baby-sitter by default. Its invasive presence deals a final blow to any lingering hope that the family can provide a sheltered space for children to grow up in.

This means the individuals who control the content of television and film are able to replace the social and moral foundation that mothers would've provided.

Who is controlling the media? In the film industry one fact is clear: people who have money have the power. It doesn't matter who wants to make a movie, nothing happens until the dollars start flowing. The executive producer, who is like the CEO for each project, is beholden to the financier who can insist upon any changes they like. Essentially they can control the content of movies. The system is ripe for conspiracy.

The current political battles between elite Liberals (who want more entitlements and a bigger government as a bridge to Socialism) and true Conservatives (who want to maintain individual autonomy) are playing out in the film industry as well. The radical political affiliation of the majority of people in the movie business is no secret. It is the same as the elite (the term 'elite' signifies how they perceive themselves) who have a virtual monopoly of all the main-stream media outlets and shamelessly use them for their own political and social agendas. Their funding is limitless and a simple tool, but it's a tool that is very effective in Hollywood. It is supremely illogical to think that the powerful and wealthy individuals who control the majority of main stream media would ignore the ripe, low hanging fruit of influence in the movie industry. Ergo, movies should at the very least be screened for themes that may undermine our personal freedom and happiness.

In her book *Shut Up and Sing*, Laura Ingram discusses the preponderance of Liberals in our film industry and concludes that either more Liberals are drawn to this line of work, or they toe-the-line by spewing liberal rhetoric in order to get work. Regardless of the reason, their agenda is firmly entrenched. In one example, Kelsey Grammer, of "Cheers" and "Frasier" fame, admitted that he may never work again in the industry because he attended George W. Bush's inauguration in 2000.

Ingram goes on to identify case after case where giants in the film industry are cozying up to Communist dictators, attacking everything about the United States and pushing more social programs that bring us closer to the Imperialistic ideals that J.P. Morgan mentioned. Ingram dismisses these people as confused lunatics who live extremely sheltered lives but it is more sinister than that. These people, these elites, knowingly follow the very purposeful guidance of their financiers and handlers who have clear goals they want to accomplish. Ingram stops one step short in her analysis, the last step being: if Sean Penn lionizes Venezuelan Communist leader Hugo Chavez on "The David Letterman Show," at the same time he is calling for the impeachment of our own president, currently George W. Bush, then Penn is advocating communism. He is not just confused or misinformed; he is following orders from his superiors–the people who pay his enormously inflated paychecks.

The movies that he chooses to work in support his political stances. Certainly Penn would never make a movie that supports the United States government, or citizens' right to bear arms. Their agenda is unmistakable, especially based on the high profile bloviating of their Hollywood pawns; it is a New World Order, with a socialist/communist/imperialistic government where the

The McCarthy hearings included a significant number of people in Hollywood for a reason: there were many communists in the movie business. Ronald Reagan, president of the Screen Actors Guild, firmly opposed the Communists in the guild without endorsing public witch-hunts and worked toward a compromise between the government and the film industry which included blacklisting those believed to sympathize and endorse communism. Incidentally, one actor whose career ended when he was named on the list was Sean Penn's father.

uber-elite have ultimate control over our lives. Penn and all the others who laud the Reds (including Warren Beatty who made the movie, *Reds*) are peddling propaganda to our impressionable families and making millions of dollars doing it. These movies mock our government, morals and conservative values in increasingly flagrant ways. Thus, they are following the dictates of the murderous dictator of the Soviet Union, Josef Stalin, when he explained, "America is like a healthy body and its resistance is threefold: its patriotism, its morality and its spiritual life. If we can undermine these three areas, America will collapse from within."

The elites' immediate goal for the United States is a lower standard of living for all citizens and a greater dependence on social programs as a bridge toward ultimate domination. For example, the website for the ultra liberal Children's Defense Fund lists pleasant sounding programs for foster care reform and children's health care that benefit needy children. These programs would have full control over people's lives and give them menial care in exchange for their freedom and independence while weakening the Federal government with even more beaurocracy and expenditures. For the beneficiaries, it creates an utter dependence on the programs and thwarts any chance of self-sufficiency. These programs also illustrate what the elite want for an ideal citizen: someone who is so hopelessly reliant on government programs, that they are unable to sustain themselves independently and therefore willing to give up even more freedoms in order to continue receiving handouts. Lenin based his vault to power selling a solution to the deplorable living conditions of the masses. In America, the Liberal Elite and Progressives are trying to create the same environment.

Accordingly, their goal in movies is to encourage lifestyles and actions that stunt potential and lead to poverty, drug addiction, low education, atheism, fragmented families and misery. Why? Because these are the people who want and need the majority of entitlement handouts. In an article about poverty on townhall.com, Bill Steigerwald interviewed Robert Rector of the Heritage Foundation on the causes of poverty in our country. Rector explains the two main reasons the official poor are poor, "One is that their parents don't work much. [16 hours per week] The second major reason that children are poor is a single parenthood in the absence of marriage." The second situation accounts for about two-thirds of all poor children. Rector continues on saying in general the families "have a whole lot of behavioral issues in addition to mere economic issues— possibly drug problems, mental problems, certainly very low work effort, probably unmarried mothers and so forth." Unequivocally, degenerated morals lead to poverty and heartache through the disintegration of the family, leaving every individual involved, particularly children, absolutely defenseless and subject to the cruel whims of society.

Tragically these destructive lifestyles are celebrated and even advocated in many movies today. Why would filmmakers or anyone else in Hollywood spend their life energy on projects that harm our citizens and weaken our country? Even if they are solely motivated by money (which is the nicest possible explanation), by exhibiting such putrescence, they should be considered equal to drug dealers who profit by destroying people's lives. Everyone involved in creating movies scrutinizes each action, theme and undertone. Nothing accidentally shows up in a film. From the first pitch of a script through the final editing process, where scenes are selected and ordered, everything is deliberate. Therefore, the rubbish is intentional and the effects on society are also intentional. The politics of the majority of the power-players in this industry complete the picture; these individuals want a more socialized government, and they advance their cause by advocating lifestyles that lead to a dependence on welfare programs that they champion.

It uncannily resembles *Star Wars I: The Phantom Menace* (1999) where Senator Palpatine paid off the Trade Federation to start a war with the Naboo. Then in a seemingly benevolent gesture he meekly offered to take charge as Supreme Chancellor to solve the problems expeditiously. He played both sides against each other to support his devious purpose of total control. EVERYONE was just a pawn to be used and discarded. He didn't care who was harmed, killed or ruined on his relentless course toward total domination of the whole empire. The enemy we face today is similarly deceptive and devious in their bid for ultimate control.

But why is the movie industry entangled in seemingly political realms? First, the system is easily controlled by those who have money. Second, this is their preferred mode of operation where they can influence public opinion while flying under the political radar. "By establishing reading societies, and subscription libraries, and taking these under our direction, and supplying them through our labors, we may turn the public mind which way we will." Of course in the days of Adam Weishaupt, front man of the Illuminati, there weren't any cinemas; if they had existed he would have surely suggested their exploitation as well. The bottom line is this: people who want to gain control of our personal freedoms have a documented history of using the arts, especially film, to influence public opinion and manipulate the masses. The conspiracy theories may or may not be true, but the subversive nature of contemporary cinema indicates the presence of subtextual agendas. Even if there is no one evil mastermind plotting to control the world, the effects of the deplorable morals in movies today lead to the same end, servitude and sorrow. The intention is irrelevant, because the outcome is the same, *nolens volens*. The Illuminati may or may not be working to subvert our society, but it is useful to study their methods because anyone endeavoring to exercise more power over any community would use the same tactics.

The Keys to Happiness, Freedom and Prosperity
CHAPTER FIVE

While we may understand how the immoral lifestyle modeled in movies and popular media will bring misery, poverty and dependency on a system that seeks to suppress us as individuals and especially as families, counteracting these destructive influences requires extra effort. This is the critical step and purpose of not only this chapter but also the whole reason for writing this book. To become an extraordinary movie viewer, you must be able to recognize and choose for yourself which values are acceptable and helpful in obtaining your own goals. Movies are a classroom for real life. Cinema can be used to uplift and inspire to greatness or to degrade and thwart hope for a positive future. We are masters who must choose for ourselves and our families, no one else should exercise that authority over us, nor should we willingly give up our individual autonomy. Through an understanding of the history of regulating morals in film, analyzing current venues for judging movies and following the Five Guidelines for Discerning Movies we will be prepared to evaluate a film's worthiness on our own.

As the film industry grew from its infancy in the early 1900's, so did the breadth of material covered. In order to deal with questionable content and determine appropriateness various groups such as the Catholic League of Decency would screen and approve or disapprove individual movies. Individual states created their own censorship regulations which led to different versions of titles being shown in different states. The ensuing chaos and continued public outrage over the reproachful behaviors like adultery, substance abuse and murder, exhibited in movies and by movie stars, lead to the creation of the Motion Picture Association of America or MPAA, (as it has been called since 1945) in an industry attempt at self regulation. The burgeoning movie business hoped to avoid government censure and improve their public image.

Previous political experience prepared Will H. Hays, the inaugural president of the MPAA, for the battles he would eventually fight in the film industry. In 1920, Hays acted as the campaign manager for President Warren Harding, a conservative Republican who ran with the slogan, "A return to normalcy," at the end of the First World War. His landslide victory over the Democratic candidate, Ohio Governor James M. Cox, who advocated a continued expansion of Roosevelt's social programs, signified the will of the American people to be more self-reliant.

The issues important to President Harding were very likely important to Hays as well. Given Hays' success, he must have been acutely aware of what the citizens of our country valued, in addition to processing awareness of the spread of morally bankrupt values that accompany socialistic governments on the international scene. When he took charge of the MPAA, he vowed that he would improve the quality films being distributed in America. Although his determination was tested, it never faltered during the eight years battle for the adoption of The Motion Picture Production Codes in 1930.

The landmark implementation of the Hays' Codes, as they became known, changed dramatically the moral content of films being shown to the American public almost overnight, lasting through the 30s 40s and 50s. Its protective shadow left with a similarly jarring jolt almost forty years later. A common misconception is that the U. S. government controlled the codes and therefore the content of movies, but this is false. The Motion Picture Association of America was entirely organized, empowered and controlled by the studios themselves. The Codes are fascinating on their own right as an analysis of the breadth and depth of influence the movie industry has.

Their aim was much more than deleting swear words and exposed bodies, the MPAA hampered harmful themes as well. The preface to the Production Codes explains their rational:

Hence, though regarding motion pictures primarily as entertainment without any explicit purpose of teaching or propaganda, they know that the motion picture within its own field of entertainment may be directly responsible for spiritual or moral progress, for higher types of social life, and for much correct thinking.

Once in place, the MPAA previewed each film released, judging it based on their guidelines. Then they would offer their approval, or not. Often times, to procure the MPAA greenlight certain words or scenes were removed from a film. Most theaters agreed to only show products that received the happy face from the MPAA. In essence, it worked like a protective parent in filtering out offensive material.

While the Hays' Codes were in place, the public could safely enjoy the movie experience without worry. Although the system was not perfect, there's no arguing that the moral quality of movies during the application of the Production Codes is higher than morals of contemporary cinema. My mother fondly remembers dressing up in Sunday best, including gloves and nylons, throughout her school years to attend the cinema in downtown Denver. Movies like *The Sound of Music* (1965), *Around the World in 80 Days* (1956) and *My Fair Lady* (1964) were true works of art that showed in theaters for months at a time. My mother recalls how she loved watching these movies over and over.

Shrill political voices proclaim that movies have no effect and they're just entertainment, yet the opposite is true. Those in the industry know this. The Hays' Codes were a part of daily life for those working in film during the Production Codes. Those who produce filth that violates these codes know what they are doing. Breaking away from the prescribed guidelines can clearly be viewed as a deliberate attempt to stifle spiritual and moral progress, spread false thinking and lower all standards.

Everything changed abruptly 1968, the year the MPAA ceased enforcing the Codes under the new direction of Jack

Valentti. Without warning, the protective filters of the Hays' Codes evaporated. It was like a priest or pastor who had been staunchly fighting obscene media for years, suddenly declares, "It's not my job anymore, and by the way here's what you've been missing." With the abrupt change to unregulated content, film makers have taken advantage of the trust of the general public that had been built up over decades. Today, many industry workers feign exemption to responsibility by appearing to fit under the umbrella of professional disinterest or artistic freedom. This is similar to the notion that school teachers are supposed to only teach the facts and not political platforms, but in actuality rarely refrain from personal commentary. Since the abolition of the Hays' Codes, the moral corruption shoved upon the unprepared public has grown exponentially.

The enormous change in regulations had a couple of effects; movie viewers inadvertently attended offensive films because they were not accustomed to screening movies for content and moral messages. At the same time the other side of the camera had been given a blank check for content. Although some would attempt to combat this change in cinema through appealing to the government, government regulated censorship is not the answer. The free market is a better tool, and the only one a free society should rely upon as proof of our liberty. If there is a low demand for offensive filth, which there is today, then the studios would likely make fewer of these types of movies. Unfortunately they don't. But if even more people refused to watch detrimental media, the production houses should eventually catch on or go bankrupt.

Currently consumers have the rating system of G, PG, etc as a token gesture from the MPAA established when they axed the Codes. (See appendix for the complete description of the ratings system.) The ratings, which are merely recommendations for age appropriateness are somewhat of a joke, and since the 1960's have been slowly losing credibility with viewers with their inconsistent application of ratings. For example, many adults are offended by PG-13 films like *King Kong* (2005) and *Lord of the Rings* (2001). Both were made by Peter Jackson and contain extremely disturbing graphic images of violence, showing human beings being killed without remorse or humanity. They are filled with mindless gore for gore's sake. Incidentally, Jackson started his career in the industry making horror films.

Even more disturbing though, are moves rated PG, which is supposed to mean parental guidance suggested, that overflow with violence, crudeness, sexually suggestive dialog and actions or have homosexual or transgendered characters. The Shrek movies are just one example, which I will discuss in depth in a later chapter.

The latest incident regarding the MPAA rating system involves a relatively insignificant controversy regarding labeling all movies that show people (or animals) smoking, rated R. This recommendation is in response to studies that prove watching characters smoke in movies influences youth to take up the habit. It conclusively points to the correlation of behaviors and actions on screen and imitation of such by viewers, particularly young viewers. However evil smoking may be, it pales in comparison to killing another person. Yet murder is represented in many PG movies as casual occurrence.

The confusion and misleading messages from the MPAA is a deliberate attempt to frustrate the public in their attempt at discerning the value of movies. While the public debates over the minutia, such as what rating should movies that show smoking receive, egregiously offensive and destructive films, which openly mock religion and marriage, such as *American Pie* (1999) and *Dogma* (1999), are glossed over. The elites who control the whole industry are not going to undermine their own power to subdue the population by pointing out which movies may be truly harmful to us.

With the MPAA ratings system in its current state, what we are left with is the thumbs up or down of a professional movie critic. These are people who are paid to write reviews for all types of media outlets. They are not political or spiritual leaders. Many times friends have confessed to me in frustration, "If the critics loved a movie I'm sure to hate it." Often I would explain that the critics were addressing technical merits, or great artistic performances, but this never changed an opinion, because reviewers consistently avoid making any moral judgment calls. Movie critics are a part of the film industry, their survival is connected to the constant stream of celluloid flowing from the production houses. I would venture that they truly enjoy movies. The more positive reviews they give, the more the media industry love them back. They would be shredded in the press and possibly fired if they started labeling films as evil, blasphemous or immoral.

Reviews for the movie *Superbad* (2007) illustrate this clearly. This movie details the quest of two boys about to graduate from high school who want to lose their virginity and in the end, they do... with each other. The themes, according to the reviews, are extremely misogynistic besides being filled with lewd language and phallic fixation. Out of all of the reviews on Rottentomatoes.com, 90% of the professional reviews were positive. This means that 90 reviewers out one hundred recommended that people watch a movie which is morally disturbing on many levels. Out of the rotten reviews only one listed the gay romance, or bromance, as a negative. That equals about one percent. One critic, Peter Bradshaw from the UK, went so far as to mock anyone who might morally object: "It's pretty crass and pretty silly, but only a puritanical grump would deny it's funny."

If nearly all the film critics endorse the movie *Superbad*, and others like it that flaunt traditional morals for the majority of Americans, it is clear that they cannot be trusted to recommend movies for people who are concerned about those issues.

Another option, the word of mouth method, of prescreening films is great if you know someone who has already seen the movie and they share similar values. However, it has a high hit and miss factor. Also, it's not always possible to tell if others are judging movies based on the same criteria as you.

So, what are we to do? Avoid the cinema altogether? Or continue to ingest the destructive filth pedaled deliberately to us? What about the true gems? The great movies of our time that bring hope for humanity through art? Movies can be inspiring, cathartic and purely delightful. They can also erode values, instill fear or threaten our humanity. This is the true dilemma.

Based solely on the current tools most readily available to viewers to try to discern which films might be worth watching like the MPAA ratings and movie reviews, it is understandable that many consumers would simply skip the theaters altogether. No significant voice in the film industry is looking out for conservative values. If they are to be preserved in our culture, we must take the responsibility into our own hands. In order to do this, we need effective tools.

I have a key to discerning movies that everyone can use for themselves to decide which movies are likely "safe" to watch and worth the financial, emotional and block of time commitment. These are the guidelines that will help you reclaim your stewardship over your destiny:

Movie Viewer Guidelines

1. Choose the morals and standards you want to live by.
2. Regulate ALL media that you and your family experience.
3. Reinforce positive influences and minimize the negative.
4. Trust your feelings.
5. Use movies to complement dreams, interests and talents.

Step 1: Choose the morals and standards you want to live by.

Before implementing any plan to regulate entertainment in your home, you must decide on the values and actions that are most important to you. For many people, myself included, this corresponds to the tenants of their religious convictions.

Other paradigms to consider are scientific research on what brings happiness.

A *Wall Street Journal Online* article titled "What's at the Heart of Happiness," by Jonathan Clements, sums up what makes people happy. More important than excessive financial resources is what people focus on—our thoughts and feelings. Additionally, married people are happier than single, even more so if their lives are secure and progressing. Further more, focusing on relationships and experiences brings more happiness than material goods. Clements explains that regardless of other factors, "We enjoy behaving virtuously." The Happiness Institute reiterates Clements' ideas and adds: setting clear goals, living healthily, focusing on strengths and living in the moment. Even a hedonistic franchise like MTV came up with similar results from the study they co-sponsored in 2007, with the elite controlled Associated Press to determine what made young people happy. They were shocked to discover that youth who abstained from sexual relations reported being happier than those who indulged. Even more distressing to them was that over 70% of those polled in an open ended questionnaire said spending time with their family brought them the most happiness. Another surprising find to the pollsters was that around half of the respondents said religion and spirituality were very important in their lives.

Basically the scientific research mirrors what most religions advocate. Happiness is a state of mind not a possession. It is not a coincidence that the same basic qualities that bring people closer to God also bring happiness. These are eternal laws that govern our souls; doing good brings happiness, doing evil brings misery.

I noticed an extremely high positive correlation between the Hays' Codes and numerous studies on what brings happiness. In a nutshell, the studies are filled with qualities and states of being such as having control of your life, feeling productive, making a difference, marriage, attending church and so forth. On the other end of the spectrum are opposite behaviors which, therefore, decrease personal happiness like poverty, loneliness, helplessness and promiscuity. Not surprisingly, these traits are the exact behaviors that people who want to take our freedom away are encouraging.

While the Hays' Codes were a wonderful system that built the trust of the American people and brought class to the medium, I do not think that reinstating the Production Codes is possible. Therefore, it is a moot point. What we can do is use these guiding principles to judge the movies we watch ourselves and with our families. The general guidelines of the Hays' Codes are simple enough to grasp, yet profound. (These are what I use to evaluate the merit of movies.)

1. No picture shall be produced that will lower the moral standards of those who see it. Hence the sympathy of the audience should never be thrown to the side of crime, wrongdoing, evil or sin.

2. Correct standards of life, subject only to the requirements of drama and entertainment, shall be presented.

3. Law, natural or human, shall not be ridiculed, nor shall sympathy be created for its violation.

Movies do not always tell the truth. One of the big lies is that living in defiance of natural or human laws can bring happiness. Peace and contentment only come through true and virtuous thoughts and actions. The danger is that movies can present iniquitous living as an ideal, which may begin to erode our inner moral compass. By focusing on the sympathy or emotions of the audience, these guidelines address the most crucial aspect of the media.

The Production Codes continue to list specific don'ts and watch outs, like: never show alcohol consumption unless necessary for the plot, and no film or episode may throw ridicule on any religious faith. They do not attempt to advocate the entire avoidance of any wrongdoing as unacceptable for cinema, just that it should be presented with the true consequences according to laws, natural and human, and that it should not be presented enticingly.

William Shakespeare and Jane Austin, arguably some of the greatest writers in our canon, are such because they strive to present the truths in life. Jane Austin fastidiously strove to represent her character's behaviors as close to real life as possible. Decades before Austin, Samuel Johnson praised William Shakespeare in his "Preface to Shakespeare" for the Bard's use of true nature in his plays. "Shakespeare is, above all writers… the poet of nature, the poet that holds up to his readers a faithful mirror of manners and of life." Even in the plays that involve the supernatural and impossible situations Johnson explains,

> …the event which he represents will not happen, but, if it were possible, its effects would probably be such

as he assigned; and it may be said that he has not only shown human nature as it acts in real exigencies, but as it would be found in trials to which it cannot be exposed.

Applied to contemporary cinema this means that stories can take place in fantastic realms of impossibility, yet impart the truths of our human existence. Additionally, celluloid art that strive to present characters accurately are more likely to receive greater success and recognition because audiences will identify with the lives on the screen.

While reading the Motion Picture Production Codes, (see the appendix), examples of how every guideline has been flagrantly violated naturally come to mind. The first item on the Codes: "[Crimes against the law] shall never be presented in such a way as to throw sympathy with the crime as against law and justice or to inspire others with a desire for imitation," seems like a prophetic warning in light of recent headlines describing how a former stripper from Alaska imitated the actions from the movie, *The Last Seduction* (1994). The femme fatale in this film coaxes her lover into killing her husband for the insurance payoff, and gets away with it. In real life, evil actions have tragic results for everyone involved, especially the man who lost his life. The stripper, who seems to have improved her life through college, marriage and motherhood, now loses everything and has been sentenced to ninety-nine years in jail. She believed the lies sold to her in the movie and in the process has ruined or ended the lives, dreams and hopes for a brighter future for numerous people, including herself.

It is of note that the Codes cover most of the tenets of the Ten Commandments, which are the most basic guidelines God has given us. However, when the Savior taught on the Mount of Olives he gave us a higher standard to strive for in the Beatitudes. These qualities which form refined and spiritual character in individuals should also be seriously considered when judging a movie. The traits Jesus advocates through promised blessings, as found in the fifth chapter of St. Matthew in the New Testament, include **meekness, thirst for righteousness, mournfulness, humility, mercy, peacemaking, enduring persecution for righteousness** and **pureness of heart**. When we as viewers watch the credits roll at the end of a movie are we inspired to strive for a more righteous life through embracing any one of these qualities? Not that all movies are bastions of spirituality, but these are ideas that should be considered when choosing entertainment.

The encouragement to pursue more noble pursuits and subdue offensive behaviors that can come through uplifting media contrasts sharply to the methods and goals of those who desire to subject society to their dominion. The forces in the media that oppose happiness are the ones that pander to the basest levels of human existence. They profit and gain power by creating a society that is ruled by their most animalistic urges, personified by ad slogans such as "Have it your way," "obey your thirst," and "Free to do what I want." (Incidentally, the last jingle is for Chase credit cards, which is rumored to be connected to the Illuminati families.)

It's not surprising that the people who want to destroy our freedom advocate lifestyles that bring misery. Instructions written by Vladamir Lenin, former dictator of the Soviet Union, before 1921, which were distributed to leaders in many nations to facilitate a world revolution illustrate this:

1) Corrupt the young, get them away from religion. Get them interested in sex. Make them superficial, destroy their ruggedness.

2) Get control of all means of publicity and thereby:

   a) Get the peoples' mind off their government by focusing their attention on athletics, sexy books and plays, and other trivialities.

   b) Divide the people into hostile groups by constantly harping on controversial matters of no importance.

   c) Destroy the people's faith in their natural leaders by holding up the latter to ridicule, contempt and obloquy.

   d) Always preach true democracy but seize power as fast and as ruthlessly as possible.

   e) Encourage government extravagance, destroy its credit, [and] produce fear with rising prices, inflation and general discontent.

   f) Foment unnecessary strikes in vital industries, encourage civil disorders and foster a soft and lenient attitude on the part of government towards such disorders.

   g) By specious argument cause the breakdown of the old moral virtues: honesty, sobriety, continence, faith in the pledged word, ruggedness.

3) Cause the registration of all firearms on some pretext, with the view of confiscating them and leaving the population defenseless.

Take a moment to ponder the Communists' methods. The battlefield is not America's borders; it is for our minds, morality and hope. All of their goals are achievable through controlling the media, especially movies, because they can affect us so deeply. Many of these tenants have already become ingrained into American pop culture; Lenin would be so proud. Continuing to accept amoral entertainment that power-hungry dictators advocate weakens individuals and nations. These are tools to help you create your personal viewing guidelines.

Step 2: Regulate ALL media that you and your family experience.

Beyond casually choosing which film to watch at the multiplex each weekend, every form of entertainment needs to be screened and regulated on two separate levels including screening for offensive language, violence and sexual content and then filtering the harmful themes. Having a cavalier attitude in regards to viewing choices is no longer an option. Therefore all movies and TV as well as other media need to be prescreened.

Parenting magazines and advocacy groups recommend checking out the shows their children are exposed to. With this method, children are choosing their own entertainment without guidance. This is not good enough in today's permissive media climate. Parents MUST be in control of all the media that their sons and daughters experience. Before watching a movie in the theater, read all the reviews and then check out parenting websites that evaluate movies specifically for age appropriateness. Movie ratings, which are mostly based on the levels of offensive language, violence, drug use and sexual content, are the first indicators of appropriate content. To filter for detrimental themes, search the reviews for questionable plot lines and characters. The second part of the book contains specific examples of what to look for.

At home use the parental control on your cable or satellite or get rid of the service entirely. Even with the controls engaged, the commercials for products and other shows can be shockingly inappropriate for family audiences. My family took the plunge and canceled our satellite subscription, it was an adjustment, but we honestly spend more time together talking, studying, playing games and reading. I treasure these moments with my family above all others, this is what life and families are about. The sixty bucks I save each month I use to purchase titles to add to our burgeoning DVD library, which I organized according to whether it is a kid movie or one for adults. My children are free to watch any movie out of their collection.

For all movies in our home collection, I love using my Clearplay DVD player. I play regular DVDs, and download programming that seamlessly skips or mutes offensive content based on the levels I set. It's perfect for those movies that are great, except for that "one scene," or the foul language. However, Clearplay can't edit out harmful themes.

Over all, this is a crucial step to protecting yourself and your family from negative influences in the media. Include the whole family in discussions regarding which movies to watch and why or why not it is acceptable. When the children know why you approve of some movies and not others, it helps them to recognize the harmful aspects of media for times when they aren't with you and prepares them for their future roles as parents. By thoughtfully selecting the media that influences your life, you are taking charge of your destiny and your posterity's future while simultaneously reducing negative effects from those who want to destroy everyone's freedom.

Step 3: Reinforce positive influences and minimize the negative.

Very few movies are either all good or all bad. After our best efforts of avoiding negative influences in movies, it's still inevitable that we will be exposed to morals and values we disagree with, *just like real life*. To maintain our control over our own lives, we should dwell on the positives. For adults and children over the age of eight, harmful influences cannot and should not be avoided entirely. (Under the age of eight, every possible effort should be taken to show correct principles in movies because young children are not mentally mature enough to fully separate real life from the images in the media.) To minimize the impact on our families of exposure to the detrimental values in movies, we need to first recognize good and evil as defined by our own standards from step one, and second, review the affects of each film on our lives.

In the current politically correct world gone amuck, there is a movement to avoid labeling anything good or bad. Public schools teach children that alternative lifestyles are just natural, neither good nor bad, instead of the truth: homosexual living destroys families and our great traditional culture. (I am not advocating discrimination or hatred against anyone based on their choices, religion or ethnic background, but it is wrong to teach children that non-traditional living arrangements are as beneficial as marriage between and man and a woman.) In Europe the media even avoids labeling terrorists as Islamic, or even using the word 'terrorist' because they might offend someone. If we fail to recognize evil then we are more likely to become a victim.

Parents MUST make judgment calls, based on their own values, in order to prepare children for the challenges they will face. Our lives upon this earth are meant to be spent with our family. God set forth this model, starting with Adam and Eve. He sends children who are unable to care for themselves so parents have time to teach them correct principles that bring happiness, spirituality and prosperity. It is a perfect system, held together by love that ensures future generations enjoy similar circumstances as their parents. If we allow the media to dictate what our children believe then we are giving away our most cherished possession, our children's futures, and failing in our most sacred responsibility. Caving to the pressure in popular culture will weaken individuals and disrupt the continuance of common sense that circulates through healthy families, but it can only happen if we willingly give up our moral stewardship over our children.

The next part of this step requires an After Movie Review or AMR. (A list of suggested questions can be found at www.movieviewerextraordinaire.com.) This is an important step because without the extra evaluation, a films message and impressions would be accepted as truth. In an open dialog with yourself, spouse or children reinforce positive behaviors and truthfully expose negative actions and attitudes based on your judgment and personal morals; this is your opportunity to teach your children what you believe.

Another part of this step is listening to the responses from your children. When my children and I were discussing a scene in *Spider Man* (2002) where a man is assaulted by muggers, my son started crying. Concerned, I gently questioned him. He replied that he had been attacked and beaten by an older child while in first grade. I had no idea of his traumatic experience, but through this dialog I was able to understand him and help him deal with that trauma. Your conversations may not be that dramatic, but it will give you an insight into what issues they are dealing with at school or other social area.

Taking the time to discuss the issues we are exposed to in movies will give us a chance to negate the sway of harmful media on our children while increasing the strength of their own values. If we are silent when children are exposed to contrary values, then we are endorsing them. This is our responsibility to us and our children; the consequences of failure are that the permissive, selfish values of the liberal elite in Hollywood will end up defining the lives of our posterity.

Step 4: Trust you feelings.

Your feelings are your best guide. When you are not positive if a movie was beneficial or injurious, how you feel after watching it is the best indicator. If there's something that doesn't feel right, and even after reading this book you're not sure what it is, don't watch it or let your children watch it. Respecting your feelings will put you in control over which values you and your family cherish and endeavor to emulate.

Many movies blur lines between right and wrong making it nearly impossible to decipher truth academically, but feelings are the ultimate key to judging merit. When you walk out of a theater or turn off the DVD player, how do you feel about life? Is your heart turned toward your spouse and children? Do you feel inspired to live a better existence? Any movie that draws us away from our families and humanity should be treated like a poison and avoided.

Feelings are also easily manipulated when watching movies. When a movie encourages values that contradict your beliefs through altering your sympathies you know of a surety that those movies are a destructive influence in your life. As part of my research for this book I watched *The Birth of a Nation* (1915), a silent, black and white production that heralded the role of the KKK in subduing the African Americans after the civil war. Even without dialog this movie was so persuasive that while watching my sympathies aligned with the hate group. This is not at all what I believe in or endorse in any way, but the movie lead to such feelings. It took some serious reflection to understand how I could root for an entity that I find morally repulsive. Had I not had a strong sense of my personal beliefs, my principles might have been permanently altered. Because my feelings turned toward beliefs that contradict my core values, I know this film is not appropriate for me or my family.

There are countless ways that films can affect us or our families. The key is to evaluate our feelings after watching a film and rate how much they correlate with our values and beliefs from Step One. To reiterate the first chapter of this book, movies can touch us on the deepest levels of our emotions; therefore extreme care must be given to ensure that this influence enhances instead of weakens our lives.

Step 5: Use movies to complement real life.

To the degree that movies can harm us, they can benefit us as well. Movies can and should be used to build upon your unique dreams and talents as well as opening the doors to new areas of interest. As a homeschooling parent I'm always on the lookout for movies that will help my children and make my job easier. When my daughter was struggling with her spelling one year, I had her watch the movie *Akeelah and the Bee* (2006), which highlights a young girl's quest to attend the National Spelling Bee. Not only did her spelling skills improve, but she was happier while studying it. The film *October Sky* (1999) similarly inspired my son in his science lessons. In another example, my husband loves to watch the movie *Rudy* (1993), whenever he is struggling to achieve any of his goals. All of these films, and many others like them, enrich our lives through watching them.

Conversely, when individuals or families are struggling in certain areas movies should be avoided that encourage harmful behavior. For example, if a marriage is going through a rocky patch, movies that encourage adultery could have very damaging effects. If there's an issue with alcohol abuse, movies that glorify imbibing would not be helpful.

Most of the time when we watch movies, we're not thinking about any of these issues because we're trying to relax and enjoy the entertainment. This is fabulous, as long as the two hours of blissful distraction do not begin to negatively affect other aspects of life, especially our freedom, family and happiness. The more we recognize how films shape our lives and practice discerning both positive and negative in films our enjoyment of movies that we judge as beneficial will increase and we will naturally begin to withdraw from movies that we deem are corrosive.

Using the Five Steps

I was on the fence about whether to allow my two older children to watch the movie *Transformers* (2007). I read many reviews and questioned people who had seen the movie to "prescreen" if it was acceptable and worthwhile for my family. Because it seemed tolerable and had a pro-military theme, (my husband is in the army) I decided the edited Clearplay version was watchable for my preteen children. We enjoyed viewing it at home and the battle against and eventual defeat of the evil Megatron resonated with my family. The personal struggle against evil is one that everyone faces in life. The film showed the good guys (the Autobots, the military and Shia Labeouf's character Sam Witwicky) conquering the DNA based robots that wanted to destroy all the humans. But they defeat Megatron by destroying the life spark, a life creating cube that came from their planet, which can represent destroying God. There is also significant screen-time devoted to Sam's quest to have a hot girlfriend, and in fact seems like his sole motivation throughout the film. When the movie was over we had a discussion on what was good in the film and what was bad. They then understood what our family position was on that film and what beliefs (killing a God-like object) we don't agree with. Overall it was a very enjoyable evening, spent with my children. The film entertained us and presented an opportunity for me as a parent to reinforce our family's values.

Through the application of these keys, understanding of historical manipulation in film and knowledge of current methods of judging cinema, individuals will become extraordinary movie viewers

Part Two
Movie Analysis

This section is designed to provide examples of how movies can be beneficial or harmful based on films that most people may have seen. As stated earlier, few films are entirely good or bad; however, these chapters will help you recognize important elements so you may make an informed decision when selecting and discussing movies.

The Big Bulls-eye Part 1: Redefining the Family
CHAPTER SIX

The attack on the most basic and fundamental unit of our society, the family, is undeniable and relentless. It comes from every possible angle in nearly every facet of life, including schools (grade school through college), the public welfare system, all popular media, children's television programming and music. Even a few organizations that label themselves churches either openly advocate alternative lifestyles or quietly approve through the ordination of gay and lesbian clergy. One of the few voices that promotes a continuance of the traditional family unit is the family itself along with some conservative churches. Reasons for the war on traditional families abound, but it boils down to any individual or group that desires to disrupt and control our civilization must first corrode the nucleus of our society—the family.

Every individual in an intact family benefits in numerous ways. A happy marriage benefits both the parents and children significantly. Harvard Professor Daniel Gilbert explains in an article from the AAP,

> Figures show that married people are in almost every way happier than unmarried people - whether they are single, divorced, cohabiting. Married people live longer, married people earn more money per capita, married people have more sex and enjoy it more. Married people seem to be happier on every dimension that you can imagine.

This is just one among numerous studies that reach the same conclusion: marriage is a blessing upon both spouses. Perhaps even more vital is the fact that effective families perpetuate themselves through shaping the rising generation.

In secure and loving homes, parents teach their children morals, attend church together, love them unconditionally, and support and shelter them from harmful influences. Mothers and fathers work together to provide positive role models as children grow from infancy to young adults, preparing them to become parents themselves. Numerous studies, including MTV's, prove that children who live with their married parents are healthier, happier and perform better in the classroom. They are less likely to experiment with harmful drugs, engage in illegal activities and drop out of school. Although no family is perfect, generally speaking children grow into adults who look and behave much like their parents.

Of course successful families do not happen by chance, they require a significant amount of effort and determination, especially in the current anti-moral climate of popular media.

In the political and social arena, the influence of our children is a highly sought after prize. Organizations (including GLAAD, Gay and Lesbian Alliance Against Defamation) are actively lobbying for a lower age of consent; if children are legally able to make their own decisions without parental oversight, then they become helpless prey for anyone who wants to attack. Many gay blogs admit this freely; they want sex with young adults and children to be legal.

Laura Ingram mentions in her book, *Shut Up and Sing*, that there are NGO's (Non-Governmental Organizations) that seek to increase children's rights. This sounds compassionate on the surface, but their intentions are far from it. The rights they want children to have are: the right to health care without parental consent (abortion), the right to access any media outlet (like porn) regardless of parental wishes and the right to full privacy from parents "spying" on them. These are direct attacks aimed at severely curtailing parents' ability to raise their children as they see fit. NGOs operate outside the laws of any country or national government, and are therefore untouchable by voters. Many focus on the UN, so they may influence several countries at once. These organizations are privately funded and receive plenty of media coverage from the mainstream media. Besides NGO's, many organizations within our own country, have declared an all-out war on the family.

The ACLU (American Civil Liberties Union) recently won one of these battles against our children. In Virginia they sued the public library system for using filters that prevented free access to pornography on the basis of freedom of speech, and won. Now, regardless of age, anyone can find the vilest filth in any public library in that great commonwealth. Of course the ACLU cannot instigate any changes without the support of activist judges. These judges are determined to wipe out all notions of religion and traditional families in every aspect of our society, including the educational system.

This battle is real. The stakes are enormous: the very fiber that not only is the basic unit for society, but also the key to happiness, wealth and good health to individuals is under siege. Naturally, movies are a major player in this war on families.

The assault on families by Hollywood hits on many different facets. The sanctity of marriage and even healthy, normal heterosexual relationships, are dismissed as antiquated and constricting. Parents in general and other family roles are undermined in every way possible.

The efforts of movies to redefine the family unit as something other than a mom, a dad and children stand out clearly in many of popular animated films of 2006 and 2007. First the Dreamworks film, *Over the Hedge* (2006), with voices performed by Bruce Willis and Gary Shandling, is a cute and very entertaining 90 minute infomercial on redefining the family. The word 'family' is used dozens of times throughout the movie but is applied to many different groups of animals. The single, unmarried male raccoon RJ (Willis) calls himself a family of one. He runs into an eclectic group of wood animals waking from hibernation who call themselves a family. There's a single female skunk, a single opossums dad and his daughter, a single male squirrel, a single male turtle, and the only traditional family unit, the porcupines. Of course the prickly mammal unit is never called a family; that designation is reserved for only alternative groups or individuals. Additionally, the main human character is an adult single female who is a successful business woman and the president of the homeowner's association. She openly mocks other women who have children by telling them to get back to their casseroles while she takes care of more important matters.

Just like the raccoon, RJ, who persuades the supposedly wild animals to indulge in junk food pilfered from humans, this movie is peddling inferior lifestyles to children. During the final scene, RJ is welcomed into the coop of creatures as a member of their family despite his harmful actions and lies. The feel good ending leaves children with the subtle thought that families can be any number of alternative options, each one weighing equally and bringing similar happiness and fulfillment. It's a two-fold attack. First the movie lowers the value of traditional marriage. Children believe the cute and sassy animals are happiest living in a non-traditional family, imbedding the seeds for future emulation. Second, the movie *Over the Hedge* elevates the importance of friendships and groups to the family level. Although this may not sound terrible, it becomes an impediment to young adults when they begin courtships for marriage. As a personal example, a close friend postponed her wedding date twice while her fiancé continued to place his friendships, even with other women, ahead of courtship and nuptials.

Sadly many children grow up in non-traditional family units, myself included; however this is not the ideal. Youth in these circumstances know this lifestyle is difficult and selling them the lie that everyone is happy regardless of parental commitment, whitewashes their trials. Children in non-traditional families need as many examples as possible of healthy, traditional families to help them create an ideal situation when they become parents themselves.

A second children's movie that mocked traditional families is the Disney animated film *Meet the Robinsons* (2007). While this was cute and had some funny scenes, the underlying themes were somewhat darker. The main character is Lewis, a young boy, who's determined to find his birth mother who left him at an orphanage when he was a baby. Not only does this movie display his real mother abandoning him without giving the underlying reasons, but Lewis is then rejected by average looking prospective adoptive parents because he's too weird. In the end he's finally adopted by the bizarre science teachers. One jitters around with a caffeine buzz and the other wears his clothes backwards.

The boy's eventual extended family in the film includes relatives who live in flower pots, an extremely obese uncle, who can barely move, and Lewis's future wife who teaches frogs to sing and play in a symphony. These are really weird characters who would have a difficult time thriving in the real world. This is harmful to impressionable minds because children watching it will identify with the main character, who is rejected by his natural mother and other traditional families. Movies such as these teach children there is no solid definition of family. This film encourages dissatisfaction with traditional families and glorifies bizarre and alternative lifestyles. Even if parents manage to maintain a traditional family, movies are teaching our children that's not where they fit in. Unfortunately there are people who may already feel that way; it is not beneficial to encourage these feelings in anyone, particularly young children. This is political correctness gone awry.

The characters in this movie have serious social problems. This film attempts to make everyone feel good about being weird by celebrating their departure from mainstream. I am not disparaging uniqueness or individuality in any way, but there are certain basic social skills that almost every successful person needs, which most of these characters are lacking. If children were to copy these behaviors, it would impede their own social development.

The Pixar/Disney film, *Cars*, (2006) featuring the voice talent of Owen Wilson as Lightning McQueen a race car, follows a similarly destructive pattern from a different angle. In this movie all the characters are cars and there are no humans, which can be interpreted as an attack on all humanity without much of a stretch. What *is* obvious is the annihilation of the family. There is a complete absence of any characters in a traditional family. The main characters are all single individuals who don't even reference their familial backgrounds. The central focus is on finding good friends and nurturing those relationships. In the beginning of the film Lightning is told he has some free tickets to give to his friends for his next race. He can't think of anyone to give them to, because all of his associations are following him for his fame. Lightning does develop a romantic interest in a Porche named Sally (Bonnie Hunt), but any mention of a permanent commitment and future offspring is noticeably absent.

A pair of mini-vans appear to be married, but they are used as a joke. They have less than a minute of screentime in the film and are shown driving around the desert lost because the male car won't ask for directions. They are not shown with children however, and so they may be married but are not a traditional family unit.

To any young child watching this movie, the message is clear: finding and nurturing good friends is what life is about when they grow up, not marriage and family. To put this into perspective, the animation from the 1970s and 80s, like the *Flintstones* and *The Jetsons*, highlighted families in vastly different settings, one futuristic and the other prehistoric. Yet the parents showed a commitment to marriage through good and bad times, the fathers supported the families by working while the mothers raised the children and managed the household. It was reassuring to see the universal application of family. Today this is almost nonexistent. Our impressionable youth are still forming their understanding of the grownup world. They face a huge cultural battle as they define their futures with every choice they make. Destructive influences should be carefully considered as they leave clear implied and subliminal messages that undermine the family.

The big lie perpetuated in these attempts to change the basic unit of the family is that alternative versions of the family bring similar contentment and prosperity. This is categorically false. The family is designed and set forth by God, beginning with Adam and Eve.

The movie *The Incredibles* (2004) is a notable foil for the anti-family movies. The family is portrayed realistically with normal family dynamics. The mom, Helen Parr/ Elastigirl (Holly Hunter) is the main care giver for the children while the dad Bob Parr/Mr. Incredible financially supports the family. The family overcomes their challenges through using their talents and working together in order to fight evil. It's beautiful. More movies should be made like *The Incredibles*, with strong cohesive families facing and conquering any obstacles that come their way.

Sadly this is not the case. The majority of family movies have clear objectives and messages which are not accidental. The filmmakers deliberately choose the plots and stories to undermine the fabric of our society. Speculation as to their motivation is endless, but the results are crystal clear. *Over the Hedge* teaches families might be important, but you can make up your own version of "family". From Meet the Robinsons children feel that they don't fit into normal families and anti-social behaviors are cool. Finally, *Cars* implies that marriage has no part of adult life whatsoever, only good friends.

Movies made for older audiences have been flaming the family for years, even generations, especially after the Movie Production codes were abolished by the MPAA. Previously movies generally adhered to the Hay's Codes which states: "The sanctity of the institution of marriage and the home shall be upheld." I believe that many of today's family films would not have been approved by the MPAA if they had to adhere to the Hays' Codes. Now that the judging of the moral merit of films is wholly up to us as individuals, we should likewise reject any movie that mocks the sacred institution of marriage.

The Big Bulls-eye Part 2: Attacking Family Roles
CHAPTER SEVEN

Every story needs conflict. A story about Lucky the butterfly having a perfect day isn't interesting. Drama depends on tension. My screenwriting professors drilled this into our heads. There must be conflict in every scene. They always pushed us saying, "What would make the tension stronger?" "Where's the conflict in happy families?" Their advice was to create tension by presenting families with extreme flaws. It's an efficient, yet cheap trick at the expense of the backbone of our great nation.

It is nearly impossible to tear a whole piece of cloth with just your hands. However, if a few threads are snipped on the edge, then the fabric easily rips into two pieces. When one role in a family fails, remaining members are weakened and far more likely to falter as well. In a similar manner, persistent trends in the movie industry today disparage the family at every chance. This vile, yet highly effective method sneaks into our lives through seemingly benign entertainment. The effect is tragic: mothers and fathers are rendered ineffective, and children, isolated from parents and siblings, are often left to care for themselves. Shatter the individual roles that form the family, like motherhood, fatherhood and the ties that connect brothers and sisters, then the other members of the family will likely fail as well.

Sibling Enemies

One easy method to develop drama in a movie or TV show is to have brothers and sisters bicker and harp at each other. Portraying siblings as rivals is so pervasive in current media that it's difficult to find products that show a positive relationship between brothers and sisters. Nearly every single TV show and movie I have watched with my children portrays brothers and sisters as mortal enemies, worthy of the cruelest barbs and deeds. After canceling cable I noticed this subtle yet jarring effect of the media on my older children, a boy and a girl, who are close in age. After a while, they began to treat each more considerately. Then we watched the Disney movie, *Freaky Friday* (2003) while staying in a hotel. I was shocked by the instantaneous transformation in their treatment of each other. Insults and sassiness, in as eloquent form as possible for my young tweens, flew out of their mouths. It was like they were competing against each other to see who could say the wittiest lines. A little light bulb popped over my head, and the correlation between the media portrayal of sibling rivalry and the behavior of my own children was clear.

The movie *Freaky Friday*, starring Lindsey Lohan and Jamie Lee Curtis, stands out as disturbing on many levels, one being sibling rivalry. Throughout the film Anna Coleman (Lohan) bickers with her younger brother, Jake, (Chad Michael Murray). In a tortuous relationship, they fight bitterly at every chance, hedging each others' goals. Even in the end when they acknowledge they really don't hate each other, they still agree to keep teasing and picking on one another. It's a twisted version of family relations.

Other examples of disturbing sibling rivalry are *Home Alone* (1990) and *Home Alone 2: Lost in New York* (1992). In the first installment, Kevin (Macaulay Culkin) is picked on incessantly by his older siblings and cousins. They call him "a disease," a "jerk" and "what the French call, les incompetent." They laugh at him when there's no cheese pizza left for him and his older brother Buzz (Devin Ratray) says he's not lucky enough for Kevin to get killed. For many, including my husband, the fighting in the family is not even noticed. The mean behavior is a device used to strengthen the tension of the story. Kevin's wish to never see his family again doesn't make sense if they get along wonderfully, but to many viewers, particularly young people, the constant criticism is felt and accepted as normal.

What's even more disturbing is that this is not portrayed as a dysfunctional family, but an affluent, traditional family; the ideal that many young people strive for. The lingering implications are that when you grow up and have the family of your dreams, everyone will be rude and argumentative and it's normal for siblings to fight.

Ideally, siblings should help, comfort and look out for other family members, from childhood to adulthood. They should be a support system and a sounding wall; a voice of reason against negative influences and bad ideas. Likewise, children and young adults who lack a familial support system are far more vulnerable to dubious influences outside the home front. As a parent, I have had to deliberately cultivate kindness with my tweens, especially when they spent time watching Nickelode-on, Cartoon Network and the Disney channels. Think about it, how many TV shows and movies that target young people have siblings getting along and looking out for each other?

The challenge came when I sought for good examples of siblings. One movie series really stood out as a functional positive example, and that is the Harry Potter franchise. Although Harry himself is an only child and his cousin is as wicked to him as possible, the Weasley family, with their seven children all take care of each other. They show genuine concern for each others' success and well being. Although they occasionally rib each other, it is never mean spirited or cruel. More importantly, they show sincere distress when one of their siblings is struggling, like when Ginny Weasley was taken into the chamber of secrets in the second Harry Potter film.

In the movie, *A Series of Unfortunate Events* (2004) with Jim Carey, the orphaned children also display genuine kindness toward each other and work symbiotically for their survival. The disturbing part of this film is how all of the adults, besides their dead parents, are either evil or complete morons.

Ineffective Adults

Ridiculing adults, especially those in parental roles, undermines traditional family values. A harmful trend in movies and other popular media is to mock the role of traditional parents and authority figures. It is not breaking news that this is a huge theme in contemporary music and the small screen. In fact it has become so pervasive that movies and shows that don't buck authority are mocked and dismissed as antiquated and bigoted. What does this say about us as a society?

The problem with this media blitz on discrediting parents is that the message is working. The negative portrayal of parents in TV shows like *Fairly Odd Parents* and *Jimmy Neutron*, not to mention *The Simpsons* and *The Family Guy*, and movies like the Cody Banks series change the perceptions of children. I notice that after a dose or two of parental roasting shows I notice my children start to feel more anxiety. They worry about things like if I'm driving the right way, or if I bought essential groceries. Even worse is when they start handing out orders to me or my husband (which we do not tolerate). I consistently focus on de-programming my children by reassuring them that Dad and I are in charge and we know how to drive and feed our family. Of course, this is the desired and obvious effect from these types of entertainment. But what may not seem so apparent is how it seems to also be undermining how parents perceive themselves.

Without a grasp on the cause of these behaviors and intentional efforts to correct them, some parents may submit to their children's false notions of a flexible or weak parental authority structure by default. This devious pitfall, encouraged in movies which show parents and adults as incapable, strengthens children's bravado and plants seeds of doubt in mothers and fathers. Further more, this disease perpetuates itself. Children who grow up ridiculing parents often become adults who have no idea how to lead a family. I believe that the growing numbers of cohabitating couples and illegitimate children is proof of this. It's against human nature to sing the praises of youth anarchy and then upon adulthood slip into traditional roles. And from personal observations, if these types of people do find themselves in authority figure roles, they struggle with enforcing the rules they were once so wont to flaunt. In essence, they are poor parents when judged by leadership and morals.

How is this manifested in movies? Any entertainment venue that has children saving the day on their own—while adults are clueless—is an offender. For example, in *A Series of Unfortunate Events*, three recently orphaned children, Klaus, Violet and Sunny Baudelaire, (Liam Aiken, Emily Browning and Kara and Shelby Hoffman) are literally on their own resisting the nefarious plans of Count Olaf (Jim Carey) who wants to kill them and take their inheritance. The adults who aren't trying to murder them are utterly incompetent to save them. Their court appointed case worker never believes the children when they tell the truth and he continually sends them back to the evil Count Olaf or other guardians who are unable to protect them.

This movie is based on a very popular children's book series and in some way must appeal to a broad market. I pondered this theme because the implications are complicated. I personally identified with the orphans who constantly faced overwhelming trials and threats. I spent a few years in foster homes as a youth and was essentially on my own from the time I was fourteen. I grew up quickly out of necessity, as do the children in *A Series of Unfortunate Events*. This aspect mimics conventional coming-of-age stories. The Baudelaire siblings in this movie behave more like grown-ups than the adults as they solve problems maturely and creatively, but it is accomplished at the expense of the image of all authority figures.

Many children will face hardships and the examples of the orphans in this movie may help; however, it also leaves viewers, especially young people, with a sense of hopelessness and isolation. They are left with the impression that parents and other adults can't help or take care of them in a real crisis. This devious effect actually turns children's hearts away from their parents, who should be the main source of support, nurture and comfort for their children. This role does not belong to their children's best friends or sports coach, and certainly not Hannah Montana or any other media personality, as some movies imply.

Another similar trend is instead of showing children coming of age, adults are returning to teen-age. Michael Medved explains this phenomenon in his book *Hollywood vs. America*.

"...[I]n traditional coming of age stories, an adolescent faces a climactic test in which he must learn to act like a man, but in this new dumbing-of-age saga, the adult can overcome a crisis only if he learns to act like a kid."

The movie *What a Girl Wants* (2003) with Collin Firth and Amanda Bynes is a clear example of advocating successful adults disregarding their professional life in favor of adolescent behavior. The story starts out with a single male British noble, close to the Royal family, having his life turned upside down when Daphne (Bynes), a teenage daughter he has never known, comes to live with him. Lord Henry Dashwood (Firth) slowly replaces his formal court life with leather pants and listening to classic rock-n-roll music, with his daughter's encouragement. In the end he gives up his seat in parliament and fully embraces the romantic bohemian lifestyle to chase his daughter and ex-wife back to the United States.

What a Girl Wants has both positive and negative examples. With movies such as this, it is critical to include an After Movie

Review, AMR, the fourth step in the Movie Viewer Guidelines, with your families in order to point out what is acceptable and expected from your children and what your family believes. I find the movie charming to watch and it does have a family reuniting in the end. This movie could have just as easily shown Firth's character reuniting with his ex-wife and keeping his professional status. Throwing away a successful and prominent livelihood does not normally lead to happiness. In that way, this movie and others like it are bent; they are selling a lie. I don't know any single woman who would like her potential husband to give up his power-job so she could support him at whatever her profession is. This film weakens the position of the father as a provider and mature responsible adult in a romantic way. Children watching this movie may have lower respect for their hard working parents and adults may subconsciously question their professional ambition. It blasts traditional family roles of the mother as the nurturer and the father as the provider, in a movie that in other ways is pro-family, unless traditional values are reaffirmed in an AMR.

The movie *Freaky Friday* is even more anti-maturity than it is anti-siblings. The lesson that the mother and daughter must "learn" in order to switch back to their correct bodies is the mother, who is shown as too uptight, has to be more like her daughter and not the other way around. In the beginning of the story it was acceptable for the daughter to disrespect her mother because she was shown as "out-of-touch" with popular culture. By the end of the film, the mother has digressed to performing in a rock band and kissing her daughter's boyfriend. The movie makes a joke out of Curtis's character embarrassing her daughter by telling her to, "make good choices," in front of classmates as she dropped her off at school. The truth is that's what good parents do, regardless of popularity.

The daughter, however, doesn't seem to acquire any maturity. Anna Coleman (Lohan) acts the same in the beginning as in the end, only all conflicts are resolved with her mother more in the end because she is "cool." The effect on viewers is to essentially question and doubt the role of mature, responsible adults. Movies like this teach children to distrust and dismiss responsible caring adults, and subliminally cause adults to doubt their authority and leadership.

There are some truths in movies where children and youth must overcome challenges on their own. This is what traditional coming of age stories are, for example *Where the Red Fern Grows* (1974, 2003) and *Iron Will* (1994). I personally faced the fallout from parents who were unable/unwilling to care for me as a young teen and sent me away. I was forced to grow up and make my own life decisions. Of course I made many preventable missteps because I learned on my own. The problem was not that my parents needed to behave more like children, they were already doing that; they needed to grow up. I am grateful for my experiences and what I learned, but it could've easily turned out much more tragically than it did. Movies that weaken the perceived roles of parents should be treated carefully. The potential damage to families far exceeds any fleeting entertainment value of such if parents do not counter the harmful messages.

Motherhood Shmotherhood

One of the more pernicious ways in which movies undermine families is through specifically attacking the venerable role of motherhood. The current standard characterization of mothers often shows them as out-of touch, frumpy, clueless or over-controlling, power hungry career witches. In today's politically correct frenzy (which is used by the elite, secular progressives to manipulate everything) mothers even avoid giving moral guidance. There are varied ways motherhood is attacked, two prominent methods involve presenting motherhood in a negative light and valuing only the financial power of women.

Many films don't even mention mothers or motherhood. Of those that show mothers, many present them in a negative light. The movie *Raising Helen* (2004) is just one example that slams traditional moms. The plot is about a very successful, career woman Helen Harris (Kate Hudson) who inherits her sister's three children instead of the other surviving sister, Jenny Portman (Joan Cusack), who is a traditional stay-at-home mom. In a letter from the children's mother explaining her choice for Helen as a guardian, she explains that Helen is more fun and spontaneous than Jenny.

Helen struggles, of course, with her new role and when she gives up her power-job it is shown as tragic. In one instance Helen's oldest charge, Audrey Davis (Hayden Panettiere) lies to her and sneaks off to the prom with a skuzzy date. Helen calls in Jenny to help her rescue Audrey. Since Helen failed as a mother the children are sent to live with Jenny and her traditional family, but they are shown as miserable there. Everyone is happy when Helen, a single mom, takes the children back to live with her in New York.

Raising Helen also makes fun of pregnancy. It touts the recent trend in Hollywood of creating "families" in ways other than giving birth. Here Helen becomes the guardian when her sister dies. The most repellent scenes in the movie are when Joan Cusack's character, who is very pregnant throughout the film, is scorned for romanticizing the miraculous experience of pregnancy. Even parents who build their families through adoption (most of whom would sell everything they own to be able to bear their own children) depend on a woman somewhere to actually give birth, and mocking the creation of life minimizes her great sacrifice. This story demeans the beautiful event of creating a new life and declares war on the traditional family.

This movie is packaged as a story about motherhood and it fails in the delivery. Children are not better off with single parents, no matter how hip or rich they are. If this is the only option, then that's another story, but this film clearly implies that traditional families are less desirable than the modern version. The big lie perpetuated here is that everyone is happier outside of traditional families, and bearing children is old fashion. Alternative parenting harms everyone involved—especially the children—and that's a fact. Most single parents struggle to support themselves and their children. Single parents face the challenge of constant child care issues in addition to the extra burden of finding a new spouse.

Another movie that targets the role of mothers is *Mona Lisa Smile* (2003). This is another instance where in a cursory glance, it doesn't seem so bad. The story is set at an all-girl's college, Wellesley, and focuses on a group of young women in the 1950's who are caught between newfound liberation and customary cultural expectations. The girls are highly influenced by their art professor, Katherine Watson, (Julia Roberts), who encourages the young women to question their values, expectations and traditions. She also teaches by example through her affair with the Italian professor, who also likes to sleep with his students.

Every woman in this movie makes different choices and logically experiences different consequences. One student, Betty Warren, (Kirsten Dunst), embraces traditional expectations when she marries during the fall semester, but quickly becomes disillusioned with her cheating husband. Joan Brandwyn (Julia Styles) is the only other character that marries and is happy. However, her liberated professor, Katherine, acts as if her marriage is the greatest tragedy because she throws away grad school and a future career to be a homemaker and raise children. Naturally this ultra feministic agenda masquerading as a story glorifies promiscuity by both sexes and supports alternative lifestyles. Although Joan defends her choice to marry and raise children, the sympathy of the audience is clearly with Katherine and her unfettered lifestyle. Every other marriage or serious heterosexual relationship is negatively portrayed. Part of the sales pitch for Katherine's liberated values is based on the fact that all the main male characters are shown as philandering liars who aren't worth the matrimonial bond.

While the cinema apparently has elevated women from archaic roles of marriage and motherhood, men seem to be digressing in many areas. The current trend, as exemplified in *Mona Lisa Smile*, is to bash males at every chance, especially if they're white.

The Optional Male

Male bashing is characterizing men to show them as incompetent, lazy, evil, stupid, purely sexually driven, irresponsible and insensitive to the exclusion of redemptive qualities. Traditionally, the role of men has been to care and provide for their families, which frequently meant higher education and specialized training. Historically and currently, males are the majority of government officials who run our country, and in wartime, our front lines are filled with men in defense of our freedom. The point is, these are very responsible roles, millions of people depend on the masculine half (as well as the feminine counterpart) to keep our country humming along.

Any entity that has their sights set on controlling our country, particularly with shady deals, has as one of their biggest fears the educated, land and gun owning alpha male protecting his family and turf. In our PC gone amuck world, it seems men are not included in the correctness part, because bashing them is almost a given. Here are a few movies where the anti-male agenda is clear.

The Disney movie, *Holes* (2003), with Shia La Beouf, based on a book by the same name leads the pack. The film follows a teenage boy, Stanley Yelnats (La Beouf) as he struggles through reform camp, run by a hard-nosed warden (Sigourney Weaver). He arrived at camp because of a series of misfortunes that seem the standard operating procedure for his family since a curse was placed on them generations ago, by another powerful woman, Madame Zeroni (Eartha Kitt). The original Stanley Yelnats lost his fortune when he was robbed by the outlaw, Kissin' Kate (Patricia Arquette). The great wealth she amasses becomes the quest for the warden and the youngest Stanley. In the end Stanley finally breaks the curse from Madam Zeroni, by rescuing her progeny; and naturally he finds the treasure.

Not only are all the strong and powerful characters women, but all of the men are at their mercy. The warden's assistants are two bumbling idiots that are utterly incompetent. Stanley's dad and grandpa are unable to succeed professionally because of the curse. The old-time men, with the exception of the Sam, a black man who quotes poetry and woes Kissin' Kate, are uneducated, rude and murderous. It is Sam's murder that nudges Kate to become an outlaw.

Even more disparaging than the pitiful male roles is the violence against males. The warden physically assaults Mr. Sir (Jon Voigt) with rattlesnake venom while he meekly cowers before her. His resulting disfigured face is used as a joke for the boys in the camp and is treated lightly in the movie. If the roles were reversed and a female was disfigured in an attack by her male employer, there's no way an audience would accept that behavior without repercussions for the attacker. For example, the movie *Unforgiven* (1992), with Clint Eastwood, is about a gunslinger that is hired to avenge a prostitute who has been disfigured. In the movie *Holes*, the physical abuse of men by a woman is treated as a non-issue.

Overall, the success of Stanley, does very little to redeem the disparaging depiction of men in this movie. Viewers are subtly saturated with feeling of distrust for men and suspicion for ambitious career women. Their confidence and faith in the positive male qualities is eroded with every viewing. These behaviors are very destructive when carried out in real life. Male bashing movies program a society to accept that women are stronger and more intelligent therefore men deserve the criticism and contempt. Categorically mocking one whole segment of society is a tool the Nazi's used against the

Jews before they started murdering them. The total elimination of the Jews became acceptable to the German society because of the media blitz against them. Likewise, Hollywood is trying to sell us a world where men are inconsequential or non-existent.

This distorted utopia is glorified by the recent Disney release, *Ice Princess* (2005). The first time I watched it I was extremely disturbed by the lack of male characters, which is hardly mentioned throughout the story. Casey Carlyle (Michelle Trachtenberg) studies the physics of figure skating for a Harvard Scholarship project. Her single mom's, played by Joan Cusack, obsession with the Ivy League School is relentless. Her father is not even mentioned, his absence is never explained. Casey is dazzled by the skating coach, another woman, who purchased the rink with the money she received from her divorce. Casey seeks for the coach's guidance despite her perpetual cheating and underhanded efforts to thwart Casey in competition. Her mother, however, detests figure skating because women are held to the "prom queen" ideal. When Casey tries to reassure her mother of her devotion she explains, "It's always been a mom and me show." In other words, a father never was part of their family unit.

Casey develops a romantic interest in Teddy, the rink Zamboni driver. He is the only male character to have more than a minute or two of screen time, the others being Casey's science teacher who tells her physics is her calling, a faculty member of Harvard who does a brief interview with Casey, and another skater's father who only complains about working two jobs to keep his daughter in competitive figure skating. In this distorted fantasy world men are good only so much as they are useful to women, like the manual labor Teddy does at the skating rink, or for money. That is it.

The final scene of this chilly film epitomizes the false utopia: the more feminine mother and masculine behaving skating coach come together in place of real parents to chart Casey's future. *Ice Princess* is perfect for Rosie O'Donnell, but not for people who want to perpetuate the traditional family, because it advocates a new type of family unit and society that doesn't include fathers.

Another example of male bashing is the movie *Daddy Daycare* (2003) with Eddie Murphy. Murphy's character, Charlie Hinton, is a failure in his professional job. So he decides to start a daycare at home that includes his son, while his wife fights the office jockeys as a lawyer. The movie is a comedy, so naturally he commits outrageous gaffes. His ineptitude contrasts the slick prestigious daycare nearby, run by Mrs. Harridan (Angelica Houston) where the children learn foreign languages and martial arts. In the end, Charlie is re-hired at his old job, but chooses to return to the daycare business with some of his buddies. The twisted feel-good ending leaves the audience happy that he has chosen to revel in domestic duties, leaving his wife to work at a real job.

Among the poop jokes and untamed children is the cheap kick in the groin, which is used for laughs. As most any male can attest, it hurts immensely in real life. It's nothing to laugh at. This is a particular peeve of many websites that expose male bashing. By laughing when a man takes a crotch hit in a movie, audiences are trained to laugh when it really happens, instead of consoling the victim. Eventually it desensitizes viewers to the point where they can disregard the very real physical pain men feel.

This effect is connected to some recent political rhetoric. In 1998, during her co-presidency days, Hillary Clinton stated at the First Ladies' Conference on Domestic Violence in San Salvador,

> Women have always been the *primary* victims of war. Women lose their husbands, their fathers, their sons in combat. Women often have to flee from the only homes they have ever known. Women are often the refugees from conflict and sometimes, more frequently in today's warfare, victims. Women are often left with the responsibility, alone, of raising the children. (emphasis added)

Yes, women make sacrifices during war, but what about the hardships of the mostly male professionals who are separated from families, sent to foreign, hostile lands where they face the daily possibility of becoming wounded, disfigured, permanently disabled or KILLED during war? Clinton's absurd tract negates all the suffering of men during war, at the same time society is being programmed to scoff at men getting hurt through the movies. This way, war is easier for her and other elites to gloss over, except when they want to use it to put in place more socialistic government programs.

Male bashing movies discredit every male, including the only perfect person who ever lived, the Savior, Jesus Christ. Portraying all men as inferior to women, evil, or inept is morally wrong and egregiously inaccurate. For our success as families, every member needs to be strong and confident. Cohesive, happy families don't happen without a confident and loving father and an involved, compassionate mother.

The movie *Nanny McPhee* (2005) is an example of a good father, Mr. Brown, (Collin Firth) trying his best to care for his family. As a widower with seven unruly children, he struggles to find a new wife before he loses the financial support from his great-aunt Adelaide. Although in the beginning he is woefully inept, he persists and with help from Nanny McPhee (Emma Thompson), he is eventually successful in his endeavor to find a wife and improve his relationship with his children.

Strong families lead to strong individuals, who then create their own cohesive families. To prepare the youth to step into responsible roles such as parenthood and breadwinner, they need to be taught how to fill those roles. The media is definitely a factor in adult cultivation, granted not the only one, but an effective role modeler nonetheless. Oprah Winfrey frequently credits the *Mary Tyler Moore Show* for inspiring her to pursue her own professional success. What behaviors, habits and standards are we advocating to our children through the TV shows and movies they watch? Whatever they are they will likely be emulated.

To sum up, movies that show adolescent behavior as an answer to any problems, attack the relationships that bind families, advocate alternative roles for family members, or show adults–particularly males–as across the board evil or stupid are selling lies and problems. Movies ought to inspire individuals to be better and work harder; at the very least they should not encourage contrary behavior. When we walk out of a movie theater we should pause to reflect on our feelings. Ideally we should feel our hearts turn toward home with our spouses, children or parents, particularly with films that are about families.

Heretics United in Cinema
CHAPTER EIGHT

Years ago, we watched the movie *Jumanji* (1995), as a family. It was the first DVD we purchased, and we enjoyed a little home movie night to commemorate the new technology. Our children were begining to prefer more non-animated films and I felt that this was a good movie for all of us to enjoy. However, I was stunned by what my kindergarten-age son asked as I tucked him into bed that night. He looked at me sincerely and questioned, "So, is God not real?" As a scripture reading, Sunday-go-to-church family, this was extremely shocking. I assured my son that the movie was fiction and God was very real. Afterwards, I pondered why a seemingly benign, PG movie could influence my son to doubt the very existence of God in one viewing. What forces would propel the film industry to deliberately produce products which dissuade people, particularly children, from their faith in God?

The people and groups who desire to enslave the populous by removing our liberty are threatened by God, because His authority is the ultimate trump card. In order to subdue a whole population, the allegiance to higher authority and adherence to morals must be destroyed. Vladimir Lenin explained it concisely, "Our program necessarily includes the propaganda of atheism." In 1920, Lenin expounded further on the Bolshevik golden rule,

> Whatever helps the world Communist revolution is good; whatever hinders it is bad. Religion, through it's insistence upon individual responsibility to the Creator of all things, interferes with the advance of world collectivism. It is, therefore, irredeemably evil.

In these statements it is clear that Lenin fears the faith in God which elevates society from mundane existence, strengthens in hardship, heals broken hearts and inspires individuals to achieve greatness among many other positive effects. Carl Marx called it the "opiate of the masses" for a reason. Faith in a divine Creator does make people happier. People feel hope. This is why every Totalitarian government either eliminates religion (China, Mongolia, the former Soviet Union, Cuba, Poland...) or they control it (like many Islamic states that impose their notions of religious law on whole countries). The threat of people who want power over us is real. In order for them to accomplish their reprehensible design of ultimate domination, they must first cut the ties to the real and only legitimate royalty–God.

Film can be used as a tool to influence and destroy the faith of God fearing people. There are many ways that this is accomplished in movies. Among some of the most egregious and persistent ways movies undermine God are by mocking religion and religious figures, depicting life with a total absence of God and religion, debasing God's power by lauding heroes with no moral aspect, and creating their own version of religion.

Mocking Religion and Religious Figures

Truly offensive films that attack everything that is sacred in religion are often easy to identify, like *The Last Temptation of Christ* (1988), with Willem Dafoe and directed by Martin Scorsese. This film explores a scenario where Christ doubts His divinity and lusts after a prostitute, Mary Magdalene. In one especially evil scene the Savior is shown watching Mary having sex with another man. This so called "artistic vision" would do nothing for viewers outside of voyeuristic titillation and planting seeds of doubt of the divine nature of the Savior, Jesus Christ. The thousands of concerned citizens that sent letters and picketed the studio demanding the movie not be released were utterly ignored. This film was recognized as evil and nipped in the bud by the movie viewers who made their votes known with their wallets.

Despite overwhelming pressure against this movie, the studio still released it, netting a huge financial loss. The domestic total box-office sales of around $4 million constitute barely one eighth of its production budget. The production executives knew it would be a fiscal disaster but brazenly continued anyway, not because they wanted to lose money, but because they were trying to harm traditional religions. The proof is in the accounting. It can be viewed as a marketing expense for anti-Christian values.

The Last Temptation of Christ also proves that many people in the film industry support the atheistic goals of those who strive to commandeer our freedoms and traditional values.

Another blow to traditional religions are movies that have priests and religious characters as villains. In *Footloose* (1984) Kevin Bacon, as Ren McCormick, faces off with a small town's reverend over a ban on dancing. The reverend (John Lithgow), who enforces the ban, is shown as overbearing, prude and antiquated which contrasts sharply with the free-spirited, fun teenagers.

Another flick of the same ilk, though different genre, is *Kingdom of Heaven* (2005), starring Orlando Bloom. When Bloom's character arrives in the Holy Land during the Crusades he discovers that all Christian knights are wicked and idolatrous. The Islamic characters are piously righteous in comparison. These films leave the impression that all men of the cloth are evil and untrustworthy. While this may be true on rare occasion, most films only focus on the negative possibilities. Viewers leave feeling all clergy aren't trustworthy because they just spent a couple of hours rooting against them.

Luckily most of the audience members for these movies are adults who already have a deep seeded core belief system that is not easily shaken. The most harmful movies are slick, family-fare that appears to be wholesome, but actually have harmful undertones and themes, like the movie *Jumanji*, mentioned at the beginning of this chapter.

Diminishing and Re-assigning God's Powers

I spent a lot of time analyzing why *Jumanji* had such a negative impact on my young son, who was five at the time. First, the world shown in this movie appears to be like our world. In reality when we face difficult situations, we often turn to prayer for help and comfort. In the Bible fantastic events happen that are comparable to the giant insects and various calamities portrayed in the movie, like the plagues of Egypt and Moses parting the Red Sea. However, the power by which these miracles were wrought is the major difference. In the Bible and in our world, God is all-powerful, in *Jumanji*, a mystical board game has power over all creatures, space and time plus the only way to survive is to obey its rules. God has no power for deliverance, nor is His help sought or mentioned by any of the characters.

A similarly anti-religious theme is to portray space exploration and other worlds that exist without God. Two movies in particular stand out as an example fo this paradigm, *Contact* (1997), with Jodie Foster, and *K-Pax* (2001), with Kevin Spacey. Both movies focus on higher states of living through space/dimensional travel and contact with beings from other places.

I loved watching the movie *Contact*, about a scientist who discovers a signal from extra-terrestrial beings and builds a machine to visit them based on instructions in their message, until the moment Eleanor Ann Arroway or Ellie (Foster) completes her excursion in space travel and finds a meaningless, whatever you want it to be existence explained by a representation of her deceased father, not her father's spirit. The representation of her father is explained through technology as Ellie attributes his image to their downloading her memory while she was passed out. Nothing in the conversation she has with her father's image even touches on God or anything of a spiritual nature; it focuses solely on the technology of the wormhole and what will happen next.

During the interviews and questioning that follows her return to earth, Ellie reiterates that there is something out there, but does not infer that it has anything to do with God. This is very subtle, yet pernicious in it's undermining of faith in God. Ellie has just been the first human to leave our galaxy and have contact with other beings and she doesn't find God there, only technology and logic.

One of the last scenes of the movie shows Ellie Leaving with her preacher boyfriend (Matthew McConaughey) and he tells the reporters that he believes Ellie and states that they are both looking for the same thing, truth. In other words, religion is bowing to science as the ultimate source for truth. The atheistically slanted ending is set by the portrayal of the outspoken preacher as a wildly psychotic guy who blows up the space travel machine before it is activated. Luckily the scientists were prepared and had built two machines. The film doesn't totally rule out Deity; however, science is clearly shown as the more enlightened of the two.

As an audience member, I was hoping the characters would discover the far reaching arm of God, and affirm traditional Judeo/Christian beliefs of resurrection and a continuance of families through the power of God. It is set up in the beginning that Ellie wants to contact her dead mother; but they don't show an afterlife at all, only other beings who take the form of her downloaded memory. This is damaging because this is presented as truth. Not literally as being based on actual events, but it is set in our modern world and the viewer is following the characters as if they could've been watching a documentary. The movie *Contact* convincingly sells itself as a real life actuality. This can easily plant seeds of doubt in the power and legitimacy of any religion, because science saves the day, while religion is either weak or psychotic.

K-Pax chronicles the story of an other-worldly visitor, Prot (Spacey), who enlightens and helps those around him. Prot is placed in a mental institute, where all the real humans are insane. Prot offers enlightened guidance to the other patients as well as his counselor. The very clear implications are that humans aren't capable of thriving on their own. But instead of leading to God, who is the only path to salvation, the film leads the audience to seek answers from aliens. Prot explains that his planet is much more advanced, so much so that they don't even need families any more.

The problem is that this is a charming, sweet movie, which lulls the viewer into feeling that there must be some truths here. It promises the audience answers for some of our most worrisome problems as Prot helps the other patients and his counselor heal his family relations. But instead of enlightening the viewers with a reaffirmation of religious views of a universe controlled by God, they crush religion by presenting a version of the universe in which God does not exist, in addition to attacking the basic structure of families.

Other movies that follow a similar structure of promising enlightenment through futuristic settings, but fall flat because the answers they present are falsehoods are *Star Wars: Episode I The Phantom Menace* (1999), *The Matrix Revolutions (2003)* and *The Last Mimzy* (2007). These movies lead with spectacles of supernatural human powers, which call to our souls as truth, because it is truth. However, they are categorically disenchanting in the end by denying the real source of power and enlightenment, God. Who felt let down or even disgusted with Qui-Gon Jinn's explanation of the Force being related to midi-chlorians, a micro-biological organism instead of connected to a higher spiritual realm? These movies, and many others, are working to destroy God by erasing Him from the existences they create.

Movies don't have to focus on religion or God to inspire and uplift. Any movie that encourages faith in unseen powers to bring about goodness is worthwhile. This naturally includes many Christmas movies and fairy God-mother stories. Also movies like *Mary Poppins* (1964), or *Nanny McPhee* where a mystical character teaches correct behavior, reinforce a pattern that encourages young people to believe in righteousness and goodness, neither of which can be explained through science.

In countless movies the lack of reference and deference to Deity and religion is conspicuous in its total absence. Often the singular acknowledgement of God is through cursing. As an audience member, I feel deeply offended by the foul language, yet at the same time relieved to know that the characters I'm investing my time in watching at least live in a world with God. The other side of the coin is the rare occasion when a character is shown on screen praying sincerely. Clint Eastwood's character, Frankie Dunn, in *Million Dollar Baby* (2004), prays as well as consults with a Catholic priest. This movie illustrates the difficult moral choices Dunn has to make when another character wants him to help her end her broken life. Regardless of this character's eventual actions, he prays earnestly and counsels with a priest before proceeding. When deference to God and religion is portrayed in movies I personally trust the characters enough to lower my guard and flow with the story. It's a much more enjoyable and cathartic experience that can lead to enlightenment in our own lives.

Heathen Heroes

Sincere prayer in movies is rare. Frequently prayer is portrayed as weak foolishness. In the movie *Pirates of the Caribbean, Dead Man's Chest* (2006), Davy Jones, a human-like creature with tentacles covering his face, usurps evil weilding ultimate control over men's lives and their souls. One scene depicts a group of captured sailors who are given a choice between death and service on his ship. Davy Jones mocks the sailor who prays fervently with his rosary beads and then kills him for sport. Davy Jones wields ultimate power in this movie—over the elements, men's lives and the consignment of souls to endless misery–these are clearly God-like powers, yet this despicable personage has no compassion or kindness, in fact he's literally heartless.

While Davy Jones is shown as the bad guy, the supposed heroes in the story, played by Orlando Bloom and Keira Knightly, seek out a voodoo witch to bring dead characters back to life. Again this power should belong to God and not to evil characters. Yet the one minor character (the one with the Rosary beads) that seems to believe in the real God is used as a joke. Additionally the British Navy members who should have been beacons of reason and law behave just as underhandedly as the pirates.

The very real feelings viewers, especially school age children, experience during and after watching the film are that traditional religion is worthless, God is inconsequential, evil and murderous people are exciting, smart and beautiful, and if you're in a jam, don't pray—go find a voodoo witch. If these ideas were taught in school, parents would demand everyone be fired. But in the name of art and entertainment, we PAY to infuse our children with these lies.

Simply put, *Pirates of the Caribbean* perpetuates the untruth that good is bad and bad is good. Don't misunderstand the point here, the world in which we live can be very cruel and punishing, sometimes evil people commit horrendous crimes, such as muder or rape and escape the consequences of the law. The Hay's Codes acknowledged how damaging this type of movie could be. Their first General Principle expressly noted that, "Hence the sympathy of the audience should never be thrown to the side of crime, wrongdoing, evil or sin." When this occurs, all aspects of society are weakened, particularly because imitation of such behaviors leads to law breaking and moral decay.

While *Pirates of the Caribbean* and *The Last Temptation of Christ* directly assaulted the divinity and power of the Son of God, other movies use more subtle methods. *Superman Returns* (2006) with Kevin Spacey and Brandon Routh, presents itself as an allegory for the Savior Jesus Christ. The intent and results are clear because of the use the word "Savior" throughout the film, however, Clark Kent (Routh) is not a particularly moral character. In this installment of the comic book hero, Kent has fathered a child out of wedlock with Lois Lane, which he discovers upon his return from a five year absence. Lane has won a Pulitzer prize for her article, "Why the World Doesn't Need Superman," and of course the villain, Lex Luthor, (Spacey) plots to kill billions of people by building a new land mass. Superman then saves the world and destroys Luthor's growing property, with some help from Lane and her fiancé. The appellation of Savior is tossed around in discussions regarding Superman's ability and desire to physically save people. The issue arises however, in the moral neutrality of Superman. Although Luthor is portrayed as evil and despicable, Superman is not his moral antithesis. He does not win by being more righteous. This film portrays him as confused and emotionally fragile, in addition to revealing his sexual relations outside of marriage.

The comparison of Superman, or any other superhero, to Christ is dubious because in the mind of an audience member the real saving power of the Savior can be confused when compared to a morally weak Superman with limited power to save people from physical death. The true gift of the Savior is the power to redeem our souls and find peace and happiness in this life as well as the next. This is a critical distinction: one is physical and temporal while the other is spiritual and eternal. The caveat to alluding to the Christ in any superhero movie is the securing of His powers of redemption to the physical realm. When tragedies and natural disasters occur in real life, without a conspicuous intervening hand of God, genuine doubt to His existence may creep in. One way to counter this effect is by discussing with children, during an AMR, the real powers of the Lord after watching these types of films.

On the opposite end of the spectrum are the rare movies that uplift and inspire. The positive influence in viewer's lives can be equally powerful, but for good instead of bad. I'm referring to the Mel Gibson film, *The Passion* (2004). Many people left this movie motivated to live a better life; I read accounts of people confessing to past crimes, including at least one murder, and an American soldier inspired to pursue adoption of a disabled Iraqi boy.

The significant spiritual impact of the movie *The Passion* upon many viewers mirrors the phenomenal box-office success. The record profits of a purely religious story surprised the establishment so that they were forced to take notice. Ideally movie makers would adjust their productions to reflect a large conservative market, but they don't. Instead, they try to sell their own version of spiritualism, the man-made gods of environmentalism.

Ersatz Religion

After shredding every truth found in bona fide religion, Hollywood offers up its own idols to be worshipped. Religious tradition in film is being replaced by ecology as the highest moral echelon.

Environmental activism is the new standard for protagonists everywhere. The recent family film *Hoot* (2006) is a chilling example of misguided morals supplanting truths. A trio of teens battle to stop construction of a new pancake restaurant on land sheltering helpless burrowing owls. In their quest to protect defenseless animals, they vandalize a construction site and a police cruiser, resist arrest and tie up the pancake franchise owner. However, in the end when the police officer realizes it was to save an endangered species, he slaps the kids on the back and thanks them for helping him out. In other words, obeying the law of the land isn't necessary if you're following the law of the environment. Protecting animals is a noble effort, but not at the expense of humans or our laws.

Hoot steps over the line of noble environmentalism when one of the teens, Mullet Fingers (not even a human name), chooses living with the animals as a homeless person over life with his mother and step sister saying, "The animals are all the family I need." In this travesty of a film, environmentalism replaces religion as the ultimate paradigm which all actions are judged, enabling the teens to disregard the law of the land as they attack "evil" capitalism. The animals and ecosystem are then elevated to a higher position replacing traditional families. It is even more contemptible because the programming message is aimed at children.

Films with older target audiences reek of eco-friendly themes as well. It's a subtle message slipped into movies like *27 Dresses* (2008). Even though the story is about weddings, only one wedding takes place in a church and that bride swears vilely when her seam comes undone. The characters mock religion by taking the Lord's name in vain and the main character says flippantly, "I'm Jesus," when asked if she has any faults.

The outstanding role model characters on the other hand, are not religious, but ecologically minded. The main character has a crush on her boss because he is the "greenest" person she's ever met. He earned her admiration by developing an ecologically friendly company. Her sister is shown as an unworthy girl-friend for her boss because she eats meat and dislikes animals. This movie attempts to falsely elevate environmentalism to spiritual realms by juxtaposing heroes who are eco-friendly with the traditionally religious ceremony of weddings.

The battle to keep our traditional religion and morality is real. The documentary *In the Face of Evil: In Word and Deed*, by Peter Schweizer, describes the colossal battle Ronald Reagan had with Communism,

> The Beast had always hated the same things: religion, a free press, intellectual inquiry, artistic expression, anything that elevated the individual and yet anyone who called out the beast were vilified, considered reactionary, paranoid, war-mongers.

Once inspiring ideals are removed from people's lives, other influences have fertile ground in which to develop. Rush Limbaugh describes this scenario in an article in his newsletter about the pseudo-religious tenor of the current global warming propaganda, "People who do not believe in God, do not become people who believe nothing, but people who will believe in anything."

It is clear that Communists and other oppressive regimes despise religion and anything that elevates and inspires individuals. An over-abundance of movies push this sickening agenda and proving Hollywood is not looking out for our religious traditions. Instead they are aiding a stealthy enemy who seeks to subdue everything that is precious, particularly our religion. We as viewers must be able to recognize these caustic messages in order to negate their influences on our families, freedom and happiness.

Putrescent Principles
CHAPTER NINE

Decaying morals is perhaps the most pernicious and extensive problem with contemporary cinema. Numerous times my family has wanted to enjoy a weekend movie, but we could not find *any* that were worth watching at the huge multiplexes. Often their schedules are filled with horror movies, like the Saw series, or super crass comedies that cater to the basest level of humanity, both of which offend the majority of Americans.

Movies that glorify promiscuity and every other imaginable form of sexual relations abound. However, numerous studies show that these behaviors don't lead to happiness or prosperity. Why then are movies pushing lifestyles and actions that harm us, and especially impressionable youth?

One of the many reasons is there are organizations that benefit from sexually promiscuous, non-married people. Among them are social programs, both government and private, for the disadvantaged, like The Children's Defense Fund and Planned Parenthood. Of these, Planned Parenthood is the most reprehensible. They are a business, not a charity or church. Concern for the bottom line is their priority, not morality or spreading happiness. They make money through providing birth control and slaughtering unborn children, which is their monumental, government funded cash cow. In order to sustain their NET PROFIT of sixty-five million dollars for the latest recorded fiscal year, they need young, unmarried girls to have more sex.

Lost Morals

The film *27 Dresses* exemplifies this problem as well. In addition to demeaning religion and God, many characters tout their loose morals and promiscuity by constantly seeking for drunken hook-ups at the wedding parties they attend. The characters who behave this way experience no negative consequences to their anti-moral behavior; in fact they openly advocate for others in the movie to emulate their actions. This is acceptable in the film because their version of spirituality does not involve morals or self control in regards to personal behavior, only strict adherence to staying "green" and following individual whims. Conservative cinematic attendees are not stupid or gullible. The movie *27 Dresses* enjoyed marginal financial success (around $70 million), but nothing compared to what similar films which espouse traditional values make, such as *My Big Fat Greek Wedding* (2002) which has grossed over $240 million, despite being an independent film.

Another example of a movie that lowers the moral standards of those who watch it is *Juno* (2007), about a sixteen-year-old who gets pregnant from a fling with a friend and gives the baby up for adoption. It encourages young people to sleep around, because the characters make it seem cool. Juno (El- len Paige) and her friend Leah (Olivia Thirlby) casually discuss sex as though it's no big deal. The movie centers around the "friendship" Juno has with the baby's father. She repeatedly denies that she has any feelings for him beyond friendship, and she just slept with him because she was bored. Throughout the movie she dismisses any possible notion of affection for the unborn child, other than deciding not to murder it. She does not want to hold the child or ever see it after the delivery. It is just an inconvenience that she's anxious to be done with.

The prevalence of non-committal sexual relations is dis- turbing and harmful to youth who watch this movie. The pro- miscuous characters in the movie *Juno* are shown as clever and interesting. When a pregnancy results from their actions, they blithely handle the pregnancy then revert to the way things were before, except that Paulie, the baby's father, and Juno, sans baby, are a couple in the end. The blatant message to young girls is that if you casually sleep with someone and get pregnant, you get the guy in the end. The startling increase in pregnant teens this past year, compared to a decade of de- crease, is proof of the effectiveness of this message.

In real life, teen pregnancy is nearly unbearable under the weight of the emotions and heartbreak. Young girls in this situation face huge losses regardless of how they choose to deal with the pregnancy. The movie sells the lie that girls who choose to place their babies for adoption don't feel any grief and that your boyfriend will love you as if nothing had hap- pened. Reality is any young woman who cares enough to de- cide not to murder her unborn child, will love that life. It is one of the laws of nature: you love what you serve and sacrifice for. She will have given up nearly a year of normal teenage life so a baby (or two) could have life. I know because I lived through it, as a fourteen-year-old in foster homes. It was the hardest time of my life, but it is also one of the experiences that I am most proud of. It made me who I am because of the challenges I faced at such a young age. It wasn't fun though. I went to my classes alone and stayed in whatever foster home I lived in at the time on the weekends. (For those who have seen this *Juno*, I did have a very rude ultra-sound technician, like in the movie.)

In contrast the film *10 Things I Hate About You* (1999), is also a high school comedy about teens navigating sexually charged relationships with similarly snappy dialog; however, they at least mention contraception and the emphasis is on building strong relationships. The boys who are worthy of affection in the end are the ones who are not just trying to get some action. While this movie shows underage drinking and plenty of sexual references, it does not advocate random sexual encounters like the film *Juno* does.

The devastating emotional toll on young girls and boys is incalculable and yet this is just one small part of the tragedy that comes from living the lascivious lifestyle echoed almost unanimously in current movies. These affects are not limited to teenagers.

In contemporary cinema, marriage frequently manifests on screen as a joke, while hot looking men and women set the standard of excitement and good times through casual sexual relations. James Bond is the classic male playboy. In every movie in the series, he "hooks up" with beautiful women and exploits them for his gain, professional and personal. He never intends to maintain a permanent relationship and has no interest in marriage. This lifestyle is a lie. Promiscuity brings heartache from dissolved unions, or the numbness of denial. Of course Bond never has to deal with unplanned pregnancies or STDs—that's not glamorous, but it is reality. What's troublesome about this series is that he is an icon for many people. The series has devoted fans who admire him, but emulation of the character's actions are anti-family in every way.

The permissive lifestyle that Bond exemplifies can lead to an increasing appetite for an intense cinematic experience. Although they are not nearly as graphic as porn films, the personal conduct of the characters in action movies is not that different.

Pornography

Pornography destroys marriages. Studies have proven that it numbs the romantic responses that occur in healthy relationships causing dissatisfaction with monogamous relations. One friend confided that although she knew her husband loved her, his addiction to porn had rendered him utterly unable to show natural affection. He also grew increasingly violent to her and their children, so that it was necessary for their safety to end the marriage.

In addition, pornography also destroys individuals. No one is better off in any way for partaking of its filth and deception. The vast majority of women do not look like or behave as the women in these films. Pornography sells images of men and women with distorted bodies, reducing their whole existence to the basest level of animalistic urges. People who pattern their behavior after porn movies often lose their families, their jobs, find themselves in jail or are designated a sex-offender for the rest of their lives. Most perniciously it turns people's hearts away from the real world and their families toward a virtual, fantasy world. In traditional marriage, men and women of every shape and size experience the true beauty of intimacy along with the emotional, physical and spiritual support, while raising children and working toward shared dreams.

With the clear destructive force on families and morals that the erotic film industry creates, it's no surprise that many political groups have taken such an interest… in ensuring that everyone has access to it. Like the ACLU lawsuit against the public libraries, Net Neutrality, a misleading euphemism for the dissemination of pornography to children, strives for the same goals. Senator Ted Kennedy explains Net Neutrality in a video posted on youtube.com advocating the right and entitlement of everyone to unrestricted high-speed internet. He supports the addiction of as many people as possible to this trash, because he advocates all the social programs that are needed when lives and families fall apart. He doesn't want to prevent the illness because he stays in power selling the cure. These mechanisms are designed to debase values, spirituality and happiness of individuals; they undermine the traditional family most of all.

In an ideal marriage intimate relations reinforce feelings of love, security and attachment between husbands and wives. This is the one area that separates the union from all other relationships. It is divinely planned as the most beautiful manifestation of love that not only creates new life, but draws couples together as one on every level. "It is the physicality of reproduction and childbirth that cements the ties between parents and children," according to Charles Fried, in his book *Modern Liberty*. He elaborates further,

> Friends of liberty must be particularly astute to discern the fallacy of those who claim that what may really be falsehood, vice, and vulgarity in sexual behavior and relations are an intrusion on their liberty to pursue the ideal.

In other words, movies that peddle filth are a direct affront on couples who seek for happiness within a monogamous marriage.

Intimacy is the core of traditional marriage, and stable families. Fried continues,

> The enemies of liberty are drawn to sex just because of its intimacy, its intensity, and because it seems to be so close to the baseline of self-ownership.

Movies are the worst offenders because they degrade this sacred and wonderful connection between husband and wife, relegating it to the realm of casual interaction without commitment or heartbreak, or even worse, an irreverent quest for horny teenagers. It is also a cheap trick in movies to show character attachments, where the writers and directors lack the skill to develop genuine emotion in more creative ways. They falsely assume that tapping into such a powerful experience/emotion in real life would translate into a powerful cinematic experience. But watching actors have sex on screen does not make a movie great. More importantly, each viewing of lewd behavior in film demeans the value of intimate relations within marriage.

The illusion here is that the very personal, sacred act of love can accurately be put on film, but it cannot. Every attempt falls short or lies. Love shown in movies, however reverently, cannot possibly include the thousands of emotions and sensations that a husband and a wife share together in real life. When individuals buy into the Hollywood version of love, they embrace a cheap imitation while giving up the authentic experience. Likewise, promiscuity, as glorified in countless films, brings sorrow not happiness.

Any outside influence that disparages the notion of sex within marriage should be treated as the greatest enemy. Any movie that makes adultery seem appealing is culpable. The stakes far outweigh the fleeting wisp of entertainment that comes from titillating cinema of every variety. Avoid them all.

Acquainting Children with the Grotesque

The elite in Hollywood know that most children are not exposed to pornography. However, there are subtle, yet disturbing methods in which movies harm our children through conditioning them to avoid making moral judgments and teaching them to embrace dubious characters. Just as portraying religious figures as corrupt weakens their image in real life, likewise showing evil or grotesque characters as appealing and good lessens children's aversion to questionable people. The truth is that there are some people that children should avoid. The liberal media often derides conservatives who make judgment calls by labeling them as homophobes or bigots. In movies this effect is most noticeable in plots that have a character that is scary and weird in the beginning, and conclude with a child discovering that they are not so bad after all.

An example of this scenario comes from the movie, *Because of Winn-Dixie* (2005), with Jeff Daniels. It's a cute family film about a young girl, Opal (AnnaSophia Robb) being raised by her preacher father after their mother walked out on them. Opal befriends a variety of unlikely characters, Pollyanna style, and makes the whole town happier along with the escapades of her mangy pooch, Winn-Dixie. However, one of her new friends is a single, adult male, fresh out of prison. They have several scenes with the two of them alone in the pet store where he works that made my skin crawl, though not because the film intends it to be questionable. Just the thought of one of my children or any other child alone with a convicted felon is unacceptable. This is not about intolerance, all people deserve kindness and courtesy, but not at the risk of the safety of any young person.

Child predators often find their victims by casually entering a child's personal space and observing their reaction. If the youth steps away, then the predator moves on. If the youth doesn't step away, then the predator proceeds to focus on the child. The tragic effects of such abuse linger for lifetimes, affecting spirituality and successful marriages. It can be devastating to instill in children the notion of befriending potentially dangerous people, like ex-convicts, mentally unstable people, weird looking old men etc. Children need to be taught to trust their feelings and instincts. It is equally important that adults respect their children's feelings and be proactive in making moral judgment calls.

Subversive Gay and Lesbian Agendas

While it seems like a no-brainer that people are generally much less likely to attend movies that are morally offensive, the majority of movies that are released fall into this category. One reason for the overabundance of cinematic filth is that private interest groups fund and promote movies based on their own agendas. The most obvious example of this is GLAAD.

GLADD and other entities are ruthless when it comes to pushing their propaganda of a gay and lesbian lifestyle onto the general population. In August 2006 GLAAD released their "Network Responsibility Index" in which it rated shows on the quality, quantity and diversity of gay characters in TV shows. The most recent ratings showed ABC, whose parent company is Disney, on top. The editor of the report, Damon Romine explains GLAAD's motives, "We know that seeing multi-dimensional, diverse people represented on television changes public perception." They also lobby film production companies heavily, insisting that more movies have gay themes and characters.

The fact that these organizations fund movies and run their own production companies allows them even greater influence. In the movie business, the people with money to fund motion pictures hold the power. Advertisements from companies seeking scripts with gay and lesbian themes abound in industry outlets. The simple reason is that anyone with a somewhat well-written script can easily secure funding for these types of movies. GLAAD and pro-homosexual groups have been so successful that they have created their own genre. Netflix, Columbia House video and Amazon are just a few of the companies to delineate the Gay and Lesbian genre.

Within the film industry gay movies are considered art. In 2006, *Brokeback Mountain*, a movie about gay cowboys, received numerous awards and nominations along with the film *Copote*, about a flamboyantly gay writer, while films that exemplify traditional values are dismissed as fanatical, out of touch or cliché. Lenin must be smiling in his grave.

The crux of this whole issue is that GLAAD wants their lifestyle to be normal and it's not. I do not hate gays. I especially do not want to force anyone to fit into any certain mold. I do want to be free to live my life, and raise my children according to traditional Christian ethics without being coerced into condoning behavior I believe is morally wrong. And every movie that portrays alternative lifestyles enticengly is a threat to my family and values.

The MPAA Production Codes took a strong stance on this issue: "Pictures shall not infer that low forms of sex relationship are the accepted or common thing." Unfortunately even children's and family films often have a customary gay character, like *Mrs. Doubtfire* (1993). When I first viewed the movie *Shrek 2* (2004), with the voice talents of Mike Meyers and Cameron Diaz, the brazenly homosexual themes astounded me. Not only is one of the characters a flaming cross-dressing bartender who openly lusts after the Prince, there were jokes about Pinocchio wearing girl's underwear. In addition to the gender confused bartender, the fairy God-mother sings a song to entice the princess to marry her son in which she cracks a whip over a cute prince as she tells her to marry a guy with a tight butt. This is teaching sexually deviant behavior to young children! The themes of this movie are not appropriate for any child or teen or adult.

As I discussed this with other parents I realized that most of them only barely noticed the man dressed as a woman and the other harmful insinuations all completely passed by under the radar, so to speak. But children watching this movie do notice. The lesson in this case is that it's funny for boys to wear girls' underwear and transvestites can't be that bad because they are in a cartoon. We should not have to explain to a four year old why a man is dressed like a woman after watching an animated film.

One specific issue that Feminists and Gay and Lesbian advocacy groups focus on is the situation of the characters in a film at the conclusion of a movie. Most often, especially for family friendly shows, a heterosexual couple draws together as part of the denouement. This is very important because when all the tensions are resolves the audience returns to a level of status quo for the characters. People who promote alternative lifestyles criticize movies that do end with a man and a women coming together. This alone is reason enough to suspect any film that does not end that way.

For example, the family film *Hoot* is about a trio of teens, two boys and a girl, trying to save endangered owls. The relationship between the boys is the focus, and neither of the boys seems interested in dating the girl, even though she's very attractive. Throughout the film Roy pursues Mullet Fingers because he is fascinated with him, then they are shown boating together. When Beatrice sneaks into Roy's room at night, there's not even a hint of romantic tension. A guy with a hot girl sneaking into his room and hiding under his bed, and he doesn't do anything? Come on! This is a dream come true for heterosexual teenage boys raging with adolescent hormones.

But the clincher for judging this to be a Gay and Lesbian themed movie is the ending: the two boys are walking along the beach together and Roy does a voice over saying that he and Beatrice became good friends

The movie *Hoot* makes my skin crawl, especially because the PG rating means that the target audience is young kids. The themes are subversion and very destructive. Children watching *Hoot* may not comprehend the harmful implications of the hidden messages and unless we counter those ideas through teaching correct principles, they will likely assimilate the lies as truth.

These are just a few ways that the big screen attempts to influence our lives. Hopefully these examples will help you recognize themes which undermine traditional values and morals in any genre. It is essential that the effects of these agenda-driven shows and others like them be minimized or eliminated from our lives, and our children's lives. Their efforts are deliberate attempts to destabilize families and religion. While the mode of attack varies widely, they all have one thing in common: they are selling a big lie that evil is good, or there is no right and wrong, only personal desires.

Movies are not just two hours of mindless entertainment as the Main Stream Media and most film critics would have you believe. Our brains and often our emotions are fully engaged. We watch movies for the same reason we read books: to learn more about life, ourselves, others and the world around us. Hollywood knows this and everyone else who's trying to influence us knows this. The motion picture industry is using it to their advantage through corrupting the moral fiber that holds our families and our country together.

Violence in Movies
CHAPTER TEN

Last year while browsing through a video rental store, a dad walked in carrying his very young daughter on his shoulders. He set her down and glanced over the new releases. Immediately the girl began desperately pleading on the verge of tears, "Please daddy, not a scary movie. PLEASE, no scary movies dad." This frightened young girl did not find violent movies entertaining, or beneficial in any way. She had evidently seen at least one horror/suspense movie in her short life which must have utterly terrified her. This innocent child did not need a critic to explain the desirability of such violent films in order to appreciate the 'art'. She also did not need to become wise to the ways of the world. I felt compassion for her and wished her dad would select an appropriate movie, although I do not know what he ultimately rented.

Violence occurs in movies of many different genres, and they are not categorically bad; however, it is critical to be able to judge which movies may have value, because some violent movies can seriously wound our spirits, or worse. The keys for discerning violence in movies fall into three categories: affects on young viewers, harmful for all viewers and acceptable for mature audiences.

Training Tots to Kill

Children are born innocent. No one comes to earth ready to murder another individual, it must be taught. When Cain was tilling the ground, he had no desire to kill until Satan tempted him with lies of promised gain through slaying his brother, Abel. Likewise, allowing young children to watch violent movies imbeds ideas of how they should behave to solve problems and creates an indifference to the suffering of others.

In 2000, a joint group of public health organizations including the American Academy of Pediatrics presented their findings on the relationship between violent movies and children's well-being at a Congressional Public Health Summit. Based on thirty years of research and over 1000 studies they stated conclusively that violent media affects children and adults negatively.

> The effect of entertainment violence on children is complex and variable. Some children will be affected more than others. But while duration, intensity, and extent of the impact may vary, there are several measurable negative effects of children's exposure to violent entertainment. These effects take several forms.

- Children who see a lot of violence are more likely to view violence as an effective way of settling conflicts. Children exposed to violence are more likely to assume that acts of violence are acceptable behavior.

- Viewing violence can lead to emotional desensitization towards violence in real life. It can decrease the likelihood that one will take action on behalf of a victim when violence occurs.

- Entertainment violence feeds a perception that the world is a violent and mean place. Viewing violence increases fear of becoming a victim of violence, with a resultant increase in self-protective behaviors and a mistrust of others.

- Viewing violence may lead to real life violence. Children exposed to violent programming at a young age have a higher tendency for violent and aggressive behavior later in life than children who are not so exposed.

These conclusions address behaviors that last throughout a child's life, in other words, they apply to adults as well.

The effects are very real, even for toddlers. For example, a few months ago, every time I picked up my two year-old son, he would wrap his hands around my neck like he was choking me. He didn't squeeze hard so it took me a couple of days to figure out that that's what he was doing. No one he is around in real-life behaves that way, so I suspected it must be a movie that he is imitating. As I mentally evaluated the recent DVD's he had seen, I remembered that there are a few scenes in the movie *The Incredibles* (2004), which my older children had been watching, where Mr. Incredible chokes another character. I explained to my older children what was happening, and that they should not watch that movie, or anything similar around him because he was learning bad habits. After that, my little guy stopped choking people.

Lt. Col Dave Grossman of the Killology Research Group explains the psychology of training our children to kill. In an article entitled "Trained to Kill," on *killology.com*, he details the harmful effects of violent media on young children.

> Something very similar to this desensitization toward violence is happening to our children through violence in the media, but instead of 18-year-olds, it begins at the age of 18 months when a child is first able to discern what is happening on television. At that age, a child can watch something happening on television and mimic that action. But it isn't until children are six or seven years old that the part of the brain kicks in that lets them understand where information comes from. Even though young children have some understanding of what it means to pretend, they are developmentally unable to distinguish clearly between fantasy and reality.
>
> When young children see somebody shot, stabbed, raped, brutalized, degraded, or murdered on TV, to them it is as though it were actually happening. To have a child of three, four, or five watch a "splatter" movie, learning to relate to a character for the first 90 minutes and then in the last 30 minutes watch helplessly

as that new friend is hunted and brutally murdered is the moral and psychological equivalent of introducing your child to a friend, letting her play with that friend, and then butchering that friend in front of your child's eyes. And this happens to our children hundreds upon hundreds of times.

This is very important because he explains very clearly that children under the age of eight are unable to understand the difference between real violence and acting. The movies they watch are even more so a classroom for how to live life, because they are in that developmental stage and are incapable of separating the entertainment value of cinema from reality. Everything is real to them.

What are young children learning by watching violent films? When they are exposed to violence through the media they may identify with the victim and feel afraid in normal situations, making it difficult to feel confident in any setting. If children do not side with the victim, then they will associate themselves with the attacker.

Regarding older children, Grossman states that violent movies, TV shows and video games are like the classic conditioning of Pavlov's dogs that associated a bell with food. Eventually they would salivate at the sound of the bell. "Our children watch vivid pictures of human suffering and death, learning to associate it with their favorite soft drink and candy bar or their girlfriend's perfume."

Another consequence of allowing any child to view graphically violent films is that they become desensitized to the suffering of people and animals. One way this issue manifests itself is as a lack of respect toward violence and death in general. Recently while watching a neighbor's five-year-old son, the boys were playing a video game that involved hunting dinosaurs with a tranquilizer. A T-rex was hit and lay sleeping on the ground, when the neighbor looked closer he dismissed the animal saying, "Where's the brain pudding? Make the brain pudding." It is tragic that any young boy would think that interacting with dinosaurs is boring unless there's blood and brains spraying from them. One can only speculate on the extent of the effects the violence he must have been exposed to at such a young age will have on his life.

The American Psychological Association has concluded after extensive research that watching violent movies and television results in an increase in similar behavior in their own life. Viewers of violent movies are more likely to be violent. This effect is so conclusive that it has a higher positive correlation than smoking and lung cancer. In other words, of the same number of smokers and individuals who watch violent films, more of the movie goers would behave violently than the number of smokers who would get lung cancer.

As a parent, a life of indifference and violence is not what I hope for and envision for my children and their posterity. I can hardly imagine a more tragic experience for them. The cause is not lost though; parents have the power to thwart these tendencies in their children by controlling the media they are exposed to. It is our right and our duty. Personally I am very choosy about what movies my children watch, and out of the ones I do green light, I filter the violence out with the Clearplay DVD player. (It's also excellent at muting offensive language.)

Movies are a classroom for life. When we sit in a theater or our living rooms at home to watch a film, our brains react to the events on screen as they would in real life, particularly young children who are not able to differentiate completely between acting and reality. Watching people murder or attack another human being or animal for entertainment instills patterns of thoughts into the minds of youth that may become actions. It is literally playing with fire. Children under the age of eight should under no circumstances be exposed to violent movies of any variety. Extreme caution should be taken regarding the violent content that older children watch.

Cinematic Terrorism

Violent movies that harm viewers most generally fall into two different categories that I base on the vastly different effects on the audience. The first type is any film that present numerous and graphic events of murder, without re-affirming the sanctity of life. These can come from many different genres, including action, drama, comedy, suspense, war, and all splatter movies. Nothing beneficial comes from viewing a movie that glorifies ending a person's life. In fact watching these types of films can have a very negative impact on the audience in various ways including desensitizing to real violence and instilling a passivity toward life in general.

The obvious and clinically proven effects connecting the watching of graphic movies to increased violence are only the tip of the iceberg. Tyrants who seek to dominate entire populations have to either conquer by force or pacify them, or a combination of both. Either way they prefer the citizens to be docile and even afraid. Movies that glorify violence lead to both.

When Vladimir Lenin swept the ruling monarchy out of Russia, he did it with only a handful of soldiers, because the general population believed his lies of a promised peace and prosperity and submitted to his rule. In order to maintain his power he brutally disposed of any potential threat to his power leading to the murder of six million people. The citizens accepted this either willingly or because they were *afraid* to fight back.

This helpless response is the exact opposite of the traditional American values. When Pearl Harbor was attacked in 1941 our people and government did not cower to the rule of the Japanese, we fought back. Likewise when the September 11 attacks occurred, our country sounded the battle cry again, because the events were shocking and tragic. In the United States, life is precious and it needs to stay that way.

Movies that revel in bloodshed and murder are a threat to our freedom because they create feelings of helplessness and apathy toward resisting evil, opening the window of opportunity for oppressive tyranny to take over. One of the ways this happens is by numbing the audience to all violence.

Michael Medved explains the effects of the current excesses in violent movies in his book, *Hollywood vs. America,*

> This higher level of tolerance for media violence may even promote acceptance of the blood-curdling cruelty we experience with increasing frequency in our own homes and communities. It is hardly a positive

development for a society when it loses its ability to feel shock.

Once citizens are no longer shocked by bloodshed, they are vulnerable to attack because the horrors of war will no longer incite a call to resist as it is associated with entertainment. They are unable to recognize and act appropriately to actual threats.

In the flurry of news coverage following the horrible shooting on the Virginia Tech school campus a few reports shed light on this correlation. Dennis Miller noted on the *O'Reilly Factor* (Apr. 18, 2007) that the only teacher to resist the murderer during the attack was a holocaust survivor, because he recognized evil. He went on to explain that the current culture does not make any judgment calls on evil things.

Watching movies like the Saw series, for entertainment, drastically diminishes a person's ability to discern what is truly evil and harmful when faced with this in real life. They have been programmed to passively watch as fellow human beings are tortured to death on screen. The gut reaction, which leads to defense and counter attack, is effectively removed.

In another report on the same incident, Ted Nugent elaborated further on CNN.com (Apr. 19, 2007), "Study the methodology of evil. It has a profile, a system, a preferred environment where victims cannot fight back." Of course he tied this in with gun control saying, "Evil is as evil does, and laws disarming guaranteed victims make evil people very, very happy. Shame on us." I add to that analysis that movies that short circuit a victim's defensive response also make evil people very, very happy.

In an interesting note concerning the effects of violent movies on viewers, the author Mark Bowden interviewed the survivors of Task Force Ranger for his 1999 best selling book *Black Hawk Down*. Through the interviews he described a unique point of view from the U.S. Army soldiers who had valiantly fought against the hordes of Somali gunmen during the 1993, two-day Battle of Mogadishu.

> Their experience of battle, unlike that of any other generation of American soldiers, was colored by a lifetime of watching the vivid gore of Hollywood action movies. In my interviews with those who were in the thick of the battle, they remarked again and again how much they felt like they were *in a movie*, and had to remind themselves that this horror, the blood, the deaths, was real. They describe feeling weirdly out of place, as though *they did not belong here,* fighting feelings of disbelief, anger, and ill-defined betrayal. *This cannot be real.* Many wear black metal bracelets inscribed with the names of their friends who died, as if to remind themselves daily that it was real.

The MPAA knew how destructive reenactments of violence could be when they wrote the Production Codes. The third general tenant states, "Law, natural or human, shall not be ridiculed, nor shall sympathy be created for its violation." And the explanation of the reasoning given in the guidelines includes the following:

> Hence the important objective must be to avoid the hardening of the audience, especially of those who are

young and impressionable, to the thought and fact of crime. People can become accustomed even to murder, cruelty, brutality, and repellent crimes, if these are too frequently repeated.

These recommendations written around seventy years ago are perhaps more applicable today than when they were written due to the increased graphic capabilities from ever-advancing special effects.

Groups or individuals who seek to dominate populations want them to be accustomed to murder, so when they violently topple governments, the citizens are not shocked, or they are too afraid to retaliate. Movies that encourage this response are ones in which the enemy is nearly undefeatable, brutal and without compassion or morals.

War of the Worlds (2005) with Tom Cruise and Dakota Fanning, epitomizes this effect. During the entire movie Ray Ferrier (Cruise) and his two children are fleeing from alien tripod robots who systematically murder humans by laser beams, which incinerate immediately or by ingesting human blood as a fuel. Throughout the movie hundreds of people are shown losing their lives, to the indiscriminate invaders. The primitive beings (humans) are utterly powerless against invaders, who are ultimately defeated through contamination by earth's germs. Based on reviews and conversations, most people were dissatisfied with this spectacle, despite the awesome special effects, but many could not elaborate why. This is why: the movie is depressing. *War of the Worlds* instills a sense of hopelessness and doubt in religion and humanity. A church is one of the first building destroyed, and after that, no mention of faith or spirituality in the face of utter extinction. Annihilating faith reinforces the despair at the fleeting and inconsequential notion of our humanity that is presented in this show. This is not only two hours of mindless entertainment, it is soulless as well. Many viewers who are not already numb to violence may find that they have to reassess their personal beliefs after this dose of Spielberg, because the message is that life means nothing. The contrived happy ending in the last minutes of the film does not negate the other two hours of horror.

Ferrier and his daughter spend the whole movie fleeing and hiding out of fear for their lives. They are shown as victims who are incapable of resisting or fighting back. Since the audience naturally identifies with the main characters, they would feel the same thing, like they are helpless victims.

Viewers who are not desensitized by extremely graphic violent films often become repulsed or afraid of violence. This leads to a climate of fear and distrust. This mirrors how terrorism works: the bad guys do something horrific, like the drug czars in Mexico beheading their enemies and throwing their heads into night clubs, so that people become afraid to cross them. Instead it is done cinematically. *War of the Worlds* and other similarly violent movies are cinematic terrorism. Extraordinary movie viewers need to be able to recognize these threats to our humanity and freedom so they can be avoided.

The Silverado Lining

Not all movies which portray violent actions are bad. Some of the most cathartic and uplifting films deal with war and other violent events. The second type of violent cinema can enrich our lives by reaffirming the sanctity of life or inspiring citizens to resist evil in all its forms (fight the bad guys).

One of my most poignant movie viewing experiences was watching the movie *Gettysburg* (1993) inside a theater in Manassas, Virginia the crisp fall day of its initial release. The large theater was filled with middle-aged men, some with dates or buddies, and others who sat alone to experience the defining battle of the Civil War. Ironically our screening was in a building that was a stone's throw or two from an actual Civil War battle field, near the green hills of the Bull Run Battlefield. The tragic story of the decimation of the Confederate Army at Gettysburg, Pennsylvania, and the bravery of men on both sides of the picket lines became our reality for the next four hours. The screenplay's vivid imagery was so realistic that it seemed jarring during the intermission to see people in modern clothing (although some individuals had on their Confederate or Union Blue caps). During the second act of the movie Col. Joshua Lawrence Chamberlain (Jeff Daniels) orders the 20th Maine men to affix bayonets and counter attack from their defensive positions because they could not repel another Rebel assault. It is a powerful scene that depicts the bravery and noble sacrifice of thousands of men. Ingrained in my mind are not the noises from the movie but the sound of dozens of grown men *sobbing* as they watched and lived this battle.

Although this magnificent film depicted the deaths of numerous soldiers, it was portrayed with respect to the scale of the human tragedy and it was done with out close ups of splattering blood or body parts. Life is sacred in the movie *Gettysburg*, as it is in reality. When many of the characters and unnamed soldiers lose their lives, the other characters, and the

audience, feel sorrow and reverence as if witnessing the tragedy in 1863.

I departed the theater with a renewed feeling of the sanctity of life and grateful for the precious freedoms we enjoy in
this country. I was also inspired to live my life more nobly and
brave, like Col. Chamberlain. It was magic.

The distinction is between movies that have violent scenes
in them to show the tragic affirmation of humanity, and films
that glorify bloodshed as entertainment. The difference can
be seen when comparing *Schindler's List* (1993) and *Saw* (2004).
While neither is appropriate for children, the first film reminds
audiences that life is sacred. After watching *Schindler's List* or
other movies like it, people normally feel imbued with a transcendent sense of purpose to their lives and caring toward others. The second movie demeans all who watch and offer zero
redemptive qualities. Subsequent to watching a movie like *Saw*
people often feel as if life is trivial and fleeting, or worse, they
may feel nudged to emulate the heinous scenes of torture and
murder.

Schindler's List is an iconic movie about helping other people
regardless of the cost. Any movie that attunes viewer's hearts
to the needs of others is beneficial in the best possible way
because they illustrate, often poignantly, ways that individuals
may reach to higher realms of existence through service. In
other words, they provide good examples to emulate.

Movies that train us to be indifferent to a person's suffering, like *Saw*, are evil not just because they thwart our natural
ability to offer help or consolation to others, but because they
crush our own soul. Charles Fried very succinctly explains the

reason we should care about the circumstances of all those around us in his book *Modern Liberty,*

> … Indifference to the suffering of others tells a story about who we are, how we regard ourselves…. The indifference expresses and teaches a disposition of the soul: a man's suffering does not matter…. The Good Samaritan is not only a neighbor to the man left half dead by thieves at the side of the road; he is neighbor—that is fellow human being—to himself.

The level of regard we have for others indicates our perceived value of all humans, including ourselves. Anyone or anything that lowers the value of life is a direct attack on our value and individual power. We should not be so careless with our souls as to accept the degrading spectacle of violent movies as mindless entertainment. Not only are our intellects weakened, but our souls as well. Conversely, movies that uphold charity for all people strengthen our spirit and resolve to live a moral life.

The other way in which some movies with violent scenes may enhance our lives is through inspiring us to resist and recognize evil. There are many classic films that show the eternal struggle to defeat the bad guys like *Braveheart* (1995), *Casablanca* (1942), *The Seven Samurai* (1954) and its remake *The Magnificent Seven* (1960), *High Noon* (1952) the original *Star Wars Trilogy* and nearly every movie with John Wayne in it. The reasons these movies are still enjoyed are because they embody the effectual struggle all humans face of choosing the right and opposing evil. These epic movies and other like them help people recognize oppression and other threats to their freedoms, families and happiness when they experience them in real life, and they implant ideas of resisting any such encroachments.

Even children's movies can exemplify these ideals. The 1998 animated Pixar/Disney film *A Bug's Life* is a good example that follows the classic hero's journey. A misfit ant, Flik, (Dave Foley) recruits circus bugs from the city to help him protect his colony from Grasshoppers who invade the island each summer to collect food the ants have collected. Flik persuades the colony to build a fake bird to scare away the invaders, but they abandon the plan when the circus bugs leave. Ultimately Flik brings the bugs back and the whole colony fights off the attacking grasshoppers, freeing their colony from oppression for good. It does have some mild animated violence, so it is not entirely suitable for very young children, but it is an excellent film for instilling a spirit of freedom even at great risk into the lives of our children.

Movies that similarly inspire are becoming increasingly rare. Many of the elite in Hollywood shun these classic story lines as cliché and archaic and instead endorse films that blur the lines between right and wrong and make the bad guys more appealing, smart and strong. Our children naturally want to be clever and attractive and will seek to emulate characters with those traits. It is critical that we chose entertainment for our children and ourselves that endorse positive values through admirable characters and actions and absolutely shun movies that instill fear and apathy through gore-filled entertainment.

I did not speak up for the little girl I watched in the video store then, but I am now. Under no conditions should a child watch violent movies and shows, especially a young child. Persons of any age would benefit from abstaining from graphic gore-fests. The consequence of failure is an increasingly violent society, desensitization to acts of violence that demean our humanity and individual worth, and a stunted ability to recognize threats of evil in life. This is the exact opposite of what children should be learning and adults should be living.

The Savior, Jesus Christ, teaches us the qualities that we should strive for in the book of St. Matthew. Blessed are the merciful: for they shall obtain mercy. Blessed are the peacemakers: for they shall be called the Children of God. And of course He gives us the two greatest commandments: Thou shalt love the Lord thy God, and thy neighbor as thyself. This should be the litmus with which we judge not only entertainment, but every thought and activity in our lives. Films that inspire us to protect and stand up for others are timeless and precious; they instill qualities that lead to prosperous and peaceful existences. Movies are the classrooms of life leading us to either good or evil. This is especially apparent in the intense emotions that accompany violent films.

Dashed Dreams
CHAPTER ELEVEN

A recent trend in movies involves undermining goals and prosperity. Customarily movies filled their roles as dream inspirations by showing the protagonists reaching for lofty goals and working to achieve them. These types of movies make up the bulk of recent classics, films over five years old that are watched repeatedly, movies that seem to never go out of style. They cross all genres with films like: *Rocky* (1976), *Goonies* (1985), *Hoosiers* (1986), *Tommy Boy* (1995), *My Fair Lady*, *Akeelah and the Bee* and *Rudy* just to name a few. Generally after watching one of these films, a person feels happy about life and their dreams. Subconsciously, or consciously, they may begin to search for long-shot goals in their own lives and start working toward them. These films form positive influences in our individual lives and society as a whole, by inspiring people to reach further, work harder and dream big.

Lately, this story type is becoming a rarity. Real ambitions are stunted by movies that glorify wishy-washy protagonists and films which saturate viewers with ambivalence toward any achievement. These films are destructive to society because they undermine dreams, hopes and achievements and plant seeds of doubt to the benefit of striving for greatness in the viewers' minds rather than affirm the desire for unequivocal success.

Low Glass Ceilings

Movies that focus on characters that have the ability to achieve their goals, but spend the entire film waffling whether they want to achieve it program viewers to doubt the validity and worthiness of their own ambitions. An obvious example of this insidious effort is the movie, *The Devil Wears Prada* (2006) with Meryl Streep and Anne Hathaway. This movie is funny and interesting to watch, with good performances and sharp dialog, in other words, it is appealing and entertaining. The problem (besides lax sexual morals) revolves around Andrea Sachs (Hathaway) and her professional dreams or lack there of. In this movie, Andrea, a couture-challenged writer, lands a one-in-a-million internship as the assistant to the editor of the biggest fashion magazine in the country. Miranda Priestly (Streep) turns out to be difficult to work with.

As Andrea struggles to succeed in the foreign world of fashion, her friends and boyfriend leave her because she spends less time with them. They don't support her or rejoice in her success, instead they selfishly complain about the time she's gone. Real friends do not cut and run when one has to work long hours or succeeds in a career, instead they support and rejoice for that friend. Sometimes, in real life, friends come and go with changes in life. It shows their shallow basis of relationships, and it is not a true loss. The fear of losing friends can be powerful, but it should NEVER be a justification for mediocrity. This movie sells a false representation, which associates fear of losing friends and relationships with professional aspiration into viewer's minds.

Andrea quickly masters the world of Miranda Priestly. The main tension of the film then switches to whether or not she will remain loyal to her previous life (ideals and friends) and her new one. In other words, it's not a movie about whether or not she can make it in the high-pressure world of fashion, but whether she wants to or not. Many people may experience flickers of doubt while climbing ambitious professional ladders, but people who eventually succeed overcome all second-guessing and push onward. While watching *The Devil Wears Prada* the audience experiences the same emotions as Andrea, which instills a fear of succeeding that is counterproductive to accomplishing dreams.

The ending is suppose to leave the audience with a happy feel-good impression when Andrea throws her job away, which she is very accomplished at, in order to write exposes on janitors' wages for small newspapers. The film makers carefully crafted the story to display how terrible life is when Andrea masters her career in a cutthroat world, and that she would be happier with meager goals and life in a very small pond. So even though she is capable, she gives it up. The very clear message to viewers is you don't really want that dream job, even though you are probably good enough to succeed, you wouldn't be happy and your friends would leave you. I don't need movies like this in my life and I certainly don't want my children watching movies that sell out their dreams.

Night at the Museum (2006) with Ben Stiller, as Larry Daley, has a similar message. The first few sequences of the movie set up how Larry is a failure in earning money, and therefore manhood. His ex-wife has custody of their son and is engaged to be married to a highly paid bond trader, the "real" man. Larry is about to be evicted from his apartment and consequently lose visitation of his son. The ex-wife makes fun of all his attempts at following his dreams by starting his own businesses throughout the movie. Then she begs him to settle for a menial hourly wage job because it will solve all his problems and make everything better.

He accepts a job at the museum where the displays come alive at night. He has a wonderful adventure and everything in his life works out. He even lands a new girlfriend all because he took a job for $11.50 an hour instead of following his entrepreneurial dreams and hopes of running his own business. What a load of trash. The American dream is based on the ability to create your own success in whatever industry you choose. This movie sells out the American dream in a fun to watch family movie.

Bee Movie (2007) with voice work by Jerry Seinfeld was even more blatant about squelching dreams of independence. It is so full of Communist propaganda Carl Marx should have been given a writing credit. The witty jokes by Barry B. Benson (voiced by Seinfeld) and cute bee scenes bled with disturbing themes of compelling the workers to stay at their one industrial job without a shard of hope for learning new talents or progressing. "You get to pick one job and do it until you die," and "It doesn't matter how stupid the job is, it is still important," are variations of lines repeated throughout the film, usually accompanied by a joke about a crud picker.

This theme is reinforced by the plot which revolves around Barry befriending a human, Vanessa (voiced by Renee Zellweger), and learning that people are profiting from their honey without compensating the bees. He then leads the bees in a lawsuit, which they win on the basis that humans are stealing from bees. After the lawsuit the bees stop production of honey resulting in total crop failure. The color drains out of the world and Vanessa, a florist, goes out of business because there aren't any flowers.

Bee Movie portrays humans very negatively, every person in the animated film, except for Vanessa, is shown as selfish morons. The bees were more enlightened, kind and interesting than the people. Vanessa's boyfriend is jealous of Barry and tries to kill him in anger; he ends up trashing Vanessa's home in the aggressive attack. The lawyer representing the honey industry is an obese back-wood's southerner who uses deceit to try to win.

In the end Barry and Vanessa steal a float from the rose parade so the bees, whose society is degrading from lack of productivity, can go back to work at their brainless, blue collar jobs, using the pollen to rejuvenate the farm and floral industry. And every one is happy.

The message to the young children watching *Night at the Museum* or *Bee Movie* is that life is ruined when you try to follow your heart or disrupt the status quo, however drudgingly that may be. It is best to just do what is expected, settle for the first blue-collar job that comes your way and get along.

Miss Potter (2006), with Renee Zellweger, is a good example of a movie that shows a young woman struggling to find her place in the world and eventually succeeding through using her own talents of writing and drawing. She fights against her stodgy parents who want her to give up her talents and marry an aristocrat. Instead she clings to her dreams, achieving literary and personal greatness.

A primary objective of any oppressive government or entity, Lenin's communist Russia for example, is to create citizens that are utterly dependent on their social programs in order that they may stay in power and so the masses are more easily managed. I am not saying that the pursuit of financial wealth should be the ultimate goal and measure of success; however citizens that enjoy a measure of prosperity have more control over their lives, i.e. freedom. Ideally pecuniary security will come through developing talents and skills that each individual enjoys. The people responsible for making *The Devil Wears Prada*, *Bee Movie* and *Night at the Museum* obviously don't have the best interest of me or my family in mind. Bill O'Reilly would say they are not looking out for families. As a parent, I want my children to do the opposite. I want them to dream the impossible dream and then work hard to achieve it. I hope that for everyone. The United States was built by people who did just that and I want to keep that option open now and for future generations.

Ambivalent Aspirations

Sports movies are a natural fit for motivational films because of the calculated odds in achieving big dreams, and there are clear goals to work for. The movie *Rudy*, with Sean Astin, will always be a family favorite. Every time we experience this story about Rudy Ruttiger (Astin) accomplishing his dream of playing for the Notre Dame football team by never wavering from his goal despite overwhelming odds including his size, academic skills, and working class background, I feel excited about life and inspired to reach further in all areas of my own life. Yet even in the sport's genre are recent movies that are undermining that dream-work-achieve process.

The movie *Annapolis* (2005) chronicles Jake Huard's (James Franco) time in the U.S. Navel Academy. In what should have been a similarly inspirational tale, when compared to *Rudy*, the audience is left scratching their heads in confusion at the lack of excitement or drive to even define his goals. Jake, who also comes from a blue collar background, is accepted into the Academy as an alternate at the last minute. Instead of being a story about his overcoming the challenges to succeed in a very competitive environment using his boxing skills, we wonder, along with the character, what he wants. Just like *The Devil Wears Prada*, the main tension is not whether or not Jake can achieve his dream, but what is his dream. So even though he has this fabulous opportunity handed to him, he waffles about whether or not it is good. The seeds of doubt are planted into the minds of the audience that attempting to live in a higher class is not worth it. Who needs that? No one. No one in a free country.

Movies with the harmful theme of advocating submission to societal class structures while they negate attempts to achieve lofty goals are multiplying at the multiplex. Through these examples, other movies that seek to squelch individual achievement can be recognized and vetted out before they harm us or our children. (Does anyone remember the movie *Invincible*?) The dreams of our children are literally a vision of the future. They need to be nurtured, not questioned, for the personal happiness of the rising generation and continuance of the freedoms we enjoy as a nation.

There is another, more subtle method Hollywood is using to curb achievement in viewers. Films that hyper-stimulate with lightening paced dialog and images, along with frantic soundtracks weaken viewer's ability to thrive in normal speed environments. Everything that is slower grows more boring. Joe Morgenstern, a reviewer for the *New York Times*, describes dismay regarding the film *Speed Racer* (2008), explaining that it "took aim at young audiences with computer-generated race car sequences of relentless intensity and incomparable incoherence." Luckily audiences generally rejected the exhibition with the wallets. However, it seems Hollywood would like to see more ADD inducing movies; labeling Speed Racer as the next big thing. Morgenstern quotes one critic in his article, "If you watch the film overwhelmed by the assault of seductive visual information and wonder what you're seeing, here's the happy answer: the future of movies." But this type of quick paced, flashing spectacle distorts the reality of our existence, which by and large thrives in a thoughtful, time managed environment. These movies harm youth and adults by creating dissatisfaction with the normal rhythms of life, and especially the long term determination and delayed gratification it takes to achieve lofty dreams.

Another way dreams are cut short is through cinema that familiarizes children with dubious lifestyles so they may begin to identify with those characters. The whole subtext of the movie *Shrek* (2001) programs children to underachieve. Shrek, the ogre voiced by Mike Meyers, saves Princess Fiona (Cameron Diaz) against her wishes because she was hoping for a prince, not an ogre. However, Shrek and Fiona begin to fall in love. A misunderstanding, stemming from a curse in which Fiona is an ogre herself at night, results in Fiona agreeing to marry Lord Farquaad, a crown seeker of short stature. Shrek returns to save Fiona and when they kiss, her curse is broken and she takes her true form… an ogre, not a princess.

Many people also look at the movie *Shrek* as a sweet love story in which outer beauty doesn't matter; that is legitimate. However the subtext is the characters are actually monstrous, instead of looking like traditional royalty, needs to be addressed if you choose to allow your children to watch this film. It can be very destructive to stunt a child's dream and hope that they are great on the inside.

As young people form ideas about life and themselves, each has to make a decision of whether they choose to follow noble and uplifting pursuits, or debasing and harmful ones. A close friend of mine who made some huge mistakes in her personal life explained it this way, "I really believed I was a terrible person and did everything possible to prove it."

On a personal note, while I was shuffled through foster homes as a pregnant fourteen-year-old, it was my faith that

God loved me and belief that I was better than my current situation that sustained me. I knew deep in my heart that I was special, despite the physical and emotional abuse from people close to me, and this enabled me to rise above the tragedies of my life and choose the blessed life I enjoy now with a wonderful husband of fifteen years and children that are loved. Without that sense of individual worth, I would've likely succumbed to the constant criticism and abuse heaped upon me.

It is pure perniciousness to destroy any child's "prince" or "princess" hope. The movie *Shrek* makes fun of traditionally noble characters like the prince and sells sympathy and admiration for the ogres. While our children are reveling in the witty banter, the seed is planted that maybe they are really an ogre, not a princess, on the inside, just like Fiona and Shrek.

If we, as parents, don't counter the negative messages in *Shrek* and other movies, we sell our children and their futures short. This stabs at one of the basic benefits of adhering to religious beliefs, the hope that inside each of us lays the kernel of greatness, through the Savior, that will bring eternal salvation.

Applications
CHAPTER TWELVE

Movies are a classroom for real life. They can be used to uplift and inspire to greatness or to degrade and thwart hope for a positive future. When the Savior, Jesus Christ, taught a principle, he did so through stories called parables, instead of giving laundry lists of do's and do not's. His parables were not for mindless entertainment, they were used to teach and provide examples for all of humanity to emulate.

Cinema presents thousands of parables with widely varying lessons for society to choose to follow. We are the masters who must select for ourselves and our families, no one else should exercise that authority over us. In review, here are the guidelines that will help you reclaim your stewardship over your destiny.

Movie Viewer Guidelines

1. Choose the morals and standards you want to live by.
2. Regulate ALL media that you and your family experience.
3. Reinforce positive influences and minimize the negative.
4. Trust your feelings.
5. Use movies to complement dreams, interests and talents.

Make a conscious choice on the values that are important, and select movies and media accordingly. The Movie Production Codes from the MPAA work best as a guide to start with. (See appendix.) Personally regulate all media that you and your family are exposed to, in your home especially. Throw out or donate movies that are harmful; don't watch them in the theater. Study the movie reviews, reading between the lines. Movies that are described with words like 'titillating', 'edgy', 'gore-fest' and 'only a puritanical grump would complain' signify the true content.

Next choose the positive values you want to accentuate and the negative ones to minimize. Reinforce positive behaviors, and truthfully expose negative actions and attitudes with an open dialog with your children, or to yourself. When a negative example does pop up, then it should be addressed immediately with a comment like, "The way they treat each other in the movie is wrong and hurtful. I'm so glad you are better than that and treat your little brother so nicely." If we are silent when children are exposed to contrary values, then we are endorsing them. This is our responsibility to our children; the consequence of failure is that the permissive, selfish values of the liberal elite in Hollywood will end up defining the lives of our posterity.

Trust your feelings about movies. If there's something that just doesn't feel right, and even after reading this book you're not sure what it is, don't watch it, or let your children watch it. Your feelings are you best guide. Respecting your feelings will enable you to choose for yourself what you want, believe and dream.

Use cinema to enhance your life. The Founding Fathers or our great nation studied almost exclusively classical literature and biographies of notable individuals, according to George Wythe in his book, *A Thomas Jefferson Education*. I believe it is possible to achieve similarly great tasks through the application their patterns to movies. Then go out and live life, real life. Enjoy the outdoors, study subjects that you are interested in, go to church, develop talents and look for ways to help others. Use movies to build upon your unique dreams, interests and talents, and to inspire you with new ideas.

Bill O'Reilly explains it succinctly in his book, *The O'Reilly Factor*,

Here's the plan. You and your family have to learn to *use the media or they will use you*. No it's worse than that. The media barons will control you. And you won't even know it. The movers and shakers of the American media don't care about you. The forces of mass

communication are directed at you; they are not designed to be an "open dialog." (emphasis added)

This book is a tool to help you to discern the influences of
the media so you can protect yourself and your family from
unwanted negative persuasion and enrich your lives with the
beauty of truth and inspiration. In the Old Testament of the
Holy Bible the prophet Joshua admonishes people to choose
whom they will serve. Purposefully selecting movies and entertainment is one way that we can choose to follow the Lord or
wicked pursuits on a daily basis. The guidelines and examples
in this book should enable readers to claim their stewardship
over their destinies and not mindlessly swallow the destructive
influences poured upon us from Hollywood. This is my hope
and prayer. God Bless.

Appendix–Documents

The Motion Picture Production Codes

(I've excluded the points that related to segregation, which was legal when this was written.)

1. Crimes Against the Law

    These shall never be presented in such a way as to throw sympathy with the crime as against law and justice or to inspire others with a desire for imitation.

    a. Murder

        i. The technique of murder must be presented in a way that will not inspire imitation.

        ii. Brutal killings are not to be presented in detail.

        iii. Revenge in modern times shall not be justified.

    b. Methods of Crime should not be explicitly presented.

        i. Theft, robbery, safe-cracking, and dynamiting of trains, mines, buildings, etc., should not be detailed in method.

        ii. Arson must subject to the same safeguards.

        iii. The use of firearms should be restricted to the essentials.

        iv. Methods of smuggling should not be presented.

    c. Illegal drug traffic must never be presented.

    d. The use of liquor in American life, when not required by the plot or for proper characterization, will not be shown.

2. Sex

The sanctity of the institution of marriage and the home shall be upheld. Pictures shall not infer that low forms of sex relationship are the accepted or common thing.

    a. Adultery, sometimes necessary plot material, must not be explicitly treated, or justified, or presented attractively.

    b. Scenes of Passion

        i. They should not be introduced when not essential to the plot.

        ii. Excessive and lustful kissing, lustful embraces, suggestive postures and gestures, are not to be shown.

        iii. In general passion should so be treated that these scenes do not stimulate the lower and baser element.

c. Seduction or Rape

> i. They should never be more than suggested, and only when essential for the plot, and even then never shown by explicit method.

> ii. They are never the proper subject for comedy.

d. Sex perversion or any inference to it is forbidden.

3. 7. Sex hygiene and venereal diseases are not subjects for motion pictures.

4. 8. Scenes of actual child birth, in fact or in silhouette, are never to be presented.

5. 9. Children's sex organs are never to be exposed.

6. Vulgarity

The treatment of low, disgusting, unpleasant, though not necessarily evil, subjects should always be subject to the dictates of good taste and a regard for the sensibilities of the audience.

7. Obscenity

Obscenity in word, gesture, reference, song, joke, or by suggestion (even when likely to be understood only by part of the audience) is forbidden.

8. Profanity

Pointed profanity (this includes the words, God, Lord, Jesus, Christ - unless used reverently - Hell, S.O.B., damn, Gawd), or every other profane or vulgar expression however used, is forbidden.

9. Costume

a. Complete nudity is never permitted. This includes nudity in fact or in silhouette, or any lecherous or licentious notice thereof by other characters in the picture.

    b. Undressing scenes should be avoided, and never used save where essential to the plot.

    c. Indecent or undue exposure is forbidden.

    d. Dancing or costumes intended to permit undue exposure or indecent movements in the dance are forbidden.

10. Dances

    a. Dances suggesting or representing sexual actions or indecent passions are forbidden.

    b. Dances which emphasize indecent movements are to be regarded as obscene.

11. Religion

    a. No film or episode may throw ridicule on any religious faith.

    b. Ministers of religion in their character as ministers of religion should not be used as comic characters or as villains.

    c. Ceremonies of any definite religion should be carefully and respectfully handled.

12. Locations

The treatment of bedrooms must be governed by good taste and delicacy.

13. National Feelings

    a. The use of the Flag shall be consistently respectful.

    b. The history, institutions, prominent people and citizenry of other nations shall be represented fairly.

14. Titles

Salacious, indecent, or obscene titles shall not be used.

15. Repellent Subjects

The following subjects must be treated within the careful limits of good taste:

1. Actual hangings or electrocutions as legal punishments for crime.
2. Third degree methods.
3. Brutality and possible gruesomeness.
4. Branding of people or animals.
5. Apparent cruelty to children or animals.
6. The sale of women, or a woman selling her virtue.
7. Surgical operations.

MPAA Guidelines for Rating Movies

(From the MPAA website)

"G" Rating, General audience, all ages admitted. A G-rated motion picture contains nothing in theme, language, nudity, sex, violence or other matters that, in the view of the Rating Board, would offend parents whose younger children view the motion picture. The G rating is not a "certificate of approval," nor does it signify a "children's" motion picture. Some snippets of language may go beyond polite conversation but they are common everyday expressions. No stronger words are present in G-rated motion pictures. Depictions of violence are minimal. No nudity, sex scenes or drug use are present in the motion picture.

"PG" Rating, Parental Guidance suggested, some material may not be suitable for children: A PG-rated motion picture should be investigated by parents before they let their younger children attend. The PG rating indicates, in the view of the Rating Board, that parents may consider some material unsuitable for their children, and parents should make that decision. The more mature themes in some PG-rated motion pictures may call for parental guidance. There may be some profanity and some depictions of violence or brief nudity. But these elements are not deemed so intense as to require that parents be strongly cautioned beyond the suggestion of parental guidance. There is no drug use content in a PG-rated motion picture.

"PG-13" Rating, Parents strongly cautioned, some material may be inappropriate for children under 13. A PG-13 rating is a sterner warning by the Rating Board to parents to determine whether their children under age 13 should view the motion picture, as some material might not be suited for them. A PG-13 motion picture may go beyond the PG rating in theme, violence, nudity, sensuality, language, adult activities or other elements, but does not reach the restricted R category. The theme of the motion picture by itself will not result in a rating greater than PG-13, although depictions of activities related to a mature theme may result in a restricted rating for the motion picture. Any drug use will initially require at least a PG-13 rating. More than brief nudity will require at least a PG-13 rating, but such nudity in a PG-13 rated motion picture generally will not be sexually oriented. There may be depictions of violence in a PG-13 movie, but generally not both realistic and extreme or persistent violence. A motion picture's single use of one of the harsher sexually-derived words, though only as an expletive, initially requires at least a PG-13 rating. More than one such expletive requires an R rating, as must even one of those words used in a sexual context. The Rating Board nevertheless may rate such a motion picture PG-13 if, based on a special vote by a two-thirds majority, the Raters feel that most American parents would believe that a PG-13 rating is appropriate because of the context or manner in which the words are used or because the use of those words in the motion picture is inconspicuous.

"R" Rating, under 17 requires accompanying parent or adult guardian. An R-rated motion picture, in the view of the Rating Board, contains some adult material. An R-rated motion picture may include adult themes, adult activity, hard language, intense or persistent violence, sexually-oriented nudity, drug abuse or other elements, so that parents are counseled to take this rating very seriously. Children under 17 are not allowed to attend R-rated motion pictures unaccompanied by a parent or adult guardian. Parents are strongly urged to find out more about R-rated motion pictures in determining their suitability for their children. Generally, it is not appropriate for parents to bring their young children with them to R-rated motion pictures.

"NC-17" Rating, no one under 17 admitted. An NC-17 rated motion picture is one that, in the view of the Rating Board, most parents would consider patently too adult for their children 17 and under. No children will be admitted. NC-17 does not mean "obscene" or "pornographic" in the common or legal meaning of those words, and should not be construed as a negative judgment in any sense. The rating simply signals that the content is appropriate only for an adult audience. An NC-17 rating can be based on violence, sex, aberrational behavior, drug abuse or any other element that most parents would consider too strong and therefore off-limits for viewing by their children.

Index